**Gene Rodde...
fans seem to
roll of stamps
writer in the**

☆☆☆

Why is STAR TREK so successful after all these years?

"...STAR TREK came along and said, 'Hey, we made it!' It's a program that says there is basic intelligence and goodness and decency in the human animal."
— *Gene Roddenberry*

☆☆☆

Do you really see STAR TREK as an accurate depiction of the Future?

"Only in the sense that we have an exciting future ahead of us..."
— *Gene Roddenberry*

☆☆☆

I like STAR TREK because Spock has green blood, and because I like the names.
— *a young fan*

☆☆☆

Gene Roddenberry did not just create a show, he created a hope.
— *Michigan viewer*

Other Ballantine Books you will enjoy:

STAR TREK LOGS ONE-NINE,
by Alan Dean Foster

THE MAKING OF STAR TREK,
by Stephen E. Whitfield & Gene Roddenberry

THE TROUBLE WITH TRIBBLES,
by David Gerrold

THE WORLD OF STAR TREK,
by David Gerrold

and

THE STAR TREK BLUEPRINTS

THE STAR FLEET TECHNICAL MANUAL

THE STAR TREK CONCORDANCE

Letters to Star Trek

edited by
Susan Sackett

with an Introduction by
Gene Roddenberry

BALLANTINE BOOKS · NEW YORK

Copyright © 1977 by Paramount Pictures Corporation

All rights reserved under International and Pan-American Copyright Conventions. Published in the United States by Ballantine Books, a division of Random House, Inc., New York, and simultaneously in Canada by Ballantine Books of Canada, Ltd., Toronto, Canada.

ISBN 0-345-25522-4-195

Manufactured in the United States of America

First Edition: January 1977

Cover art by Joseph Csatari

To Gene . . . my mentor,
For believing in me

Contents

	Foreword	1
	Introduction **by Gene Roddenberry**	5
Chapter One	**STAR TREKmania**	9
Chapter Two	**The Universal Appeal**	33
Chapter Three	**The Collector**	67
Chapter Four	**The Stars and Their Characters**	75
Chapter Five	**A Fan Is Born**	91
Chapter Six	**STAR TREK and Education**	111
Chapter Seven	**The Big Screen**	157
Chapter Eight	**Who, What, Where, When, Why, and How Come?**	177
Chapter Nine	**Dreams for a Future**	189
	Appendix	209
	Acknowledgments	213

Foreword

"STAR TREK fans seem to have been born with a roll of stamps in one hand and a typewriter in the other!"

Gene Roddenberry, creator and executive producer of the television phenomenon known as STAR TREK, has often said this to the large crowds attending his college lectures. And it is no exaggeration. STAR TREK receives several thousand letters a year, arriving at a variety of addresses: Paramount Pictures, Lincoln Enterprises, NBC (New York and Burbank offices), Filmation Studios, the STAR TREK Welcommittee, viewers' local television stations, and even *other* networks which never ran the show! No other television show current or past can claim such a fan following as STAR TREK. And, considering the fact that the show has been in rerun sydication for six years (its original network run lasted from 1966 to 1969), one asks the question: Why?

I myself can't say; it's just as much a mystery to me as it is to the studio executives and the network brass, who never dreamed such a thing would happen. There has to be only one answer: STAR TREK was and is a good television program. And there are all kinds of books, theses, and even college courses devoted to in-depth study of STAR TREK, analyzing episodes, dissecting characterization, debating philosophical concepts, and so on.

For nearly two years I have had the privilege of working closely with Gene Roddenberry as his personal executive secretary. In addition to enjoying such good fortune as being the first one to know what ideas are germinating in that fascinating mind of his, I have

Susan Sackett and friend at the Movieland Wax Museum.

also had the opportunity to read and answer more fan mail than I ever dreamed existed—often a thousand letters a week. Most secretaries would probably have turned in their typewriters by now. Not this one.

At mail call, you can usually walk into my office to find me giggling over the latest outrageously funny letter, or contemplating the daily lesson in morals, ethics, sociology, or basic science that has been suggested by some eager STAR TREK fan. All secretaries should have such interesting mail! And, of course, such an interesting boss. As one letter writer put it:

```
Dear Susan Sackett (You lucky girl
           being secretary to
The Great Bird of the Galaxy) . . .
```

She was right!

For this book I've collected many of the best fan letters—the humorous, the sad, the curious, the mind-bending. I'd like to share them not only with the STAR TREK fans who helped make this book a reality, but with anyone who enjoys a chuckle, a bit of nostalgia, or a glimpse at what some people in this world think our future will be like. Then, too, this book is our chance to respond to many of the thousands of letters and questions we just can't answer individually.

The pen is mightier than the phaser. Keep those cards and letters coming!

Susan Sackett,
Burbank, California
March, 1976

Gene Roddenberry at his desk in the Paramount Studios. A photo of Majel Barrett (Nurse Chapel of Star Trek), Gene's wife, can be seen on the shelf above.

Introduction

by Gene Roddenberry

All television shows get fan mail. In most cases, it consists mainly of letters of affection to the actors or requests for autographs or photos. Although some actors will insist on personally answering their own fan letters, more often the mail is simply counted each month by the studio to determine whether the series' popularity is growing or dropping. If any reply is sent to the fans, it usually consists of a standardized postcard acknowledgment.

In the fall of 1966, when STAR TREK went on the air, none of us making the show bothered to inquire about fan mail. All of the television critics had blasted our series in their television columns, and I think we probably feared that any letters from the audience might be saying much the same thing.

It was Isaac Asimov, the famous science-fiction writer, who changed this for us. Rather annoyed, he sent a message to our office saying that he had taken the time and trouble to write us his comments on the show and he did not particularly appreciate that the only reply he received was a machine-autographed picture of Mr. Spock. I was properly mortified, highly apologetic, and also considerably relieved to learn that his comments had been congratulatory in nature. On inquiry, I learned that the studio sent all of its television mail to an outside firm specializing in acknowledging fan mail with picture-postcard replies. Not only was Asimov right, but the same kind of reply was probably bothering other people, too. In fact, the STAR TREK mail was unlike any fan letters I had ever seen before. A surprising amount of it came from college students, teachers, and professional people—there was a letter from an engineer at NASA, a long explanation of antimatter from a theoretical physicist, and even a collection of excellent space sonnets from a poet. A lot of the mail was from children, but much of that contained interesting comments and questions which clearly deserved an intelligent reply.

As a result, the STAR TREK office staff and actors began to handle their own mail. Then, as the growing volume made it impossible for us to personally answer every letter, a specialized STAR TREK fan-mail service was organized and staffed with people who knew the show intimately.

Ten years have passed, and the volume of mail is as great as ever. Almost everyone prominently associated with STAR TREK still has to set aside time every day to answer those letters which appear to deserve a personal reply. We try to handle the rest with mimeographed forms where routine answers seem sufficient, and by sending the latest STAR TREK news out to be disseminated by fan clubs and fan magazines. There has been no studio budget for this; we've borne the cost ourselves during the almost seven years since the series was dropped by the network. We do it because we hope it will be helpful to our careers to have an audience that remains interested in our work. But we also do it because of the kinds of letters you will read in this book.

A major portion of the mail workload has always been carried by office staff. We have been particularly fortunate in the quality of people who have managed the STAR TREK offices over the years. Everyone knows that Dorothy (D. C.) Fontana went from our front desk to become story editor of the series and is now a well-known television and film writer in her own right. Anita Doohan, who handled that desk during our last production year, is now a motion-picture producer and vice-president of a large film company. Susan Sackett, the editor of this book, has been publishing on her own for more than two years now and will undoubtedly have someone managing her office someday.

I suspect that as the years go by the same success will greet many of our young fans. The quality of certain letters indicates that exciting futures await their authors. I suppose it is even possible that I'll walk into a studio or network office someday and find that the company president there is someone who once wrote STAR TREK a fan letter. Hey, wouldn't that be nice!

Gene Roddenberry discussing plans for the movie.

Chapter One

Star Trekmania

> Plees wud you tell me wiy
> you tock <u>Star</u> <u>Trek</u> off the arr?
> —Six-year-old boy
> from Florida

He was one of the lucky ones who had made it through the mob. Downstairs, the police had been called to quell the riots in the lobby. It was the largest STAR TREK convention held to date—a crowd estimated at between twenty thousand and fifty thousand people storming the New York Hilton Hotel on January 24, 1976.

The boy felt an object on the table in the dealers' room of the convention. "What's this?" he asked his father.

"It's an IDIC, son. Like Mr. Spock sometimes wears on STAR TREK. A triangle and a circle together . . ."

I'd heard it a hundred times that day. I was a guest speaker at the Con, but, due to the heavy crowds, I had found myself lending a hand at the Lincoln Enterprises table. I paid only slight attention to the pair, a father and his son, until I noticed the father take the boy's small hand and pass it over the next object for sale—a small gold model of the *Enterprise* on a chain. Then I realized that the boy was blind.

"Ooh, the *Enterprise!*" he squealed in joyful recognition.

"Yes," replied the father, with patience and wisdom. "And these are smaller IDICS," he continued as he guided the young fingers, "and these are picture postcards of the *Enterprise*. One postcard shows it crossing the galaxy barrier. The other shows the *Enterprise* in the blue sky over the Earth in 'Tomorrow Is Yesterday.'"

"May I have the IDIC and the two pictures, please?" The child's voice projected in my direction. The father handed over the money, which I took absently, and then they were again swallowed by the crowd.

"My God!" I thought. "The boy bought pictures!"

At least I had managed to hold back the tears until after the pair had gone. They were not tears of pity, but of happiness. The boy was not blind after all: he just couldn't see. Suddenly I realized what it all meant —the STAR TREK magic, the STAR TREK dream, the STAR TREK*mania*. It took a small blind boy to open *my* eyes to all that had been going on around me for the nearly two years I had been working as secretary to Gene Roddenberry, STAR TREK's creator. I was beginning to appreciate some of the closeness, the sense of "belonging," the optimism that is currently taking STAR TREK from the realm of a phenomenon toward becoming a cult in the near-religious sense of the word.

A week before, on the other side of the continent, STAR TREK had been making headlines of another sort. After a long absence from Los Angeles television, STAR TREK had its "premiere"—on a local independent station—nearly ten years after its debut on the NBC network (September 8, 1966). The program *killed* all the other stations in the ratings, including the prime-time network programs. Gene received the following letter from Jerrell Birdwell, Station KTLA's Director of Program Administration:

```
                              KTLA
                              5800 Sunset Boulevard
                              Hollywood, CA 90028
                              January 16, 1976
Mr. Gene Roddenberry
Paramount Pictures
5451 Marathon Street
Hollywood, California 90038
```

Re: <u>Star Trek</u>

Dear Gene:

<u>Star Trek</u> lives on! Enclosed is a rating summary for KTLA's special <u>Trek</u> presentation last Sunday.

Thank you very much for your help.
Sincerely,
Jerry Birdwell
Director of
Program Administration

Included with the letter was a release which disclosed the following ratings:

Movie for a Sunday Evening Special:
Star Trek "Menagerie"
Is *Number One* in the Time Period!!

KTLA re-introduces *Star Trek* to the Los Angeles market with the highest rating ever recorded in syndication in L.A.: a *14.3*!!

Sunday, January 12th 6–8 PM time period	*Rating*	*Share*
KTLA *Star Trek* "Menagerie"	14.3	24%
KABC	11.8	19%
KNXT (CBS)	11.4	19%
KNBC	9.5	15%
KTTV	4.6	7%
KHJ	4.5	7%
KCOP	4.5	7%

With the tremendous popularity of *Star Trek*, KTLA is sure to establish the best ratings ever for the series in L.A.!

They were certainly starting out right. Translating these Neilsen figures reveals some startling information. For example, there are 38,000 homes per rating point. Multiplying STAR TREK's rating of 14.3 by 38,000, we get approximately 543,000 *homes* in the Greater Los Angeles area tuned to STAR TREK! (The "share" figures refer to the percentage of television sets tuned in at the time.) The following week the station ran the episode "Where No Man Has Gone Before." It received a 13.5 rating and a 31 percent share!

Nor is Los Angeles atypical. Rather, the same sort of figures can be boasted by nearly every television station across the nation now broadcasting the syndicated program. In a survey done by Paramount Television Marketing Research in late 1975, Arbitron and/or Neilsen figures in key cities were as follows:

City	Station	Rating	Share, %	Women (18–49) (in 1000s)	Men (18–49)
Albuquerque	KOB-TV	13	52	20	25
Austin	KVUE-TV	11	34	–	–
Baltimore	WJZ-TV	–	–	35	–
Cincinnati	WXIX-TV	–	–	35	37
Denver	KOA-TV	11	33	35	–
Indianapolis	WLWI-TV	–	–	36	34
Lansing	WILX-TV	12	30	22	15
Minneapolis	WTCN-TV	5	26	27	–
New York	WPIX	–	–	202	242
(New York total homes = 501,000					
" " " persons = 943,000)					
Providence	WJAR-TV	8	26	23	–
Richmond	WTVR-TV	6	49	–	–
Sacramento	KTXL	–	–	36	47
San Francisco	KTVU	10	20	107	98

In every case, STAR TREK was *number one* in its time period, and in many cities it was on its twelfth or thirteenth run! STAR TREK is obviously alive and well and living on in reruns.

Nevertheless, there were those who loved STAR TREK in its early days who thought the world had ended when NBC killed the series in 1969. The University of South Alabama Science Fiction Club, sponsored by Dr. Ernest Roberts, Professor of Psychology, wrote:

When news of the cancelling of Star Trek reached us, our first instinct was to run out and put the flag at half-mast on the university flagpole. We hate to lose an "old intergalactic friend."

Network executives are still shaking their heads in disbelief, while the phoenixlike television show seems to have no end to its success in sight. Why is STAR TREK so successful today? Why wasn't it ten years ago, when it all started? According to Gene Roddenberry, STAR TREK's creator, there are a couple of reasons.

"First of all," says Roddenberry, "when STAR TREK

Gene Roddenberry addresses The Star Trek Convention in New York City (1975). Photo by Jeff Maynard.

was first on the air in its network run, we were just getting into space. When we made our first episode, we hadn't even been to the moon; only toward the end did people begin to accept space. Also, as we ventured into space, reputable scientists such as Carl Sagan and others began writing on the possibility of extraterrestrial life. Over a period of four or five years, the whole world's eyes were turned toward space and the possibility of things such as we were doing on STAR TREK. In most people's minds science fiction had been rather a comic-book fantasy thing. During the time that STAR TREK was leaving the air and getting into its first few reruns, the public's eyes were finally beginning to turn toward space, and science fiction became more legitimate. Science fiction has really moved into the mainstream of literature."

Fans tried to console themselves with the problems of living in a STAR TREKless world. But real despair was avoided, and no eulogy was necessary, because of STAR TREK's rebirth through syndication. There was a rebirth for many of its most active fans, too, a kind of "baptism by television." STAR TREK fans often find the need to communicate this experience, almost the way those new to a religion are frequently its most fervent proselytes. Virginia Walker, active in the STAR TREK Welcommittee (more on that later), describes her "conversion":

> Beginning in October of '73, everything in my life blew up in my face.
> Within the space of eight weeks, I lost everything I had. My wallet got lifted in Boston. A week later in New York it was my whole pocketbook—including keys and addressbook—locking me out of my home, office, car, cutting me off from my friends. The following week, my fiancé was killed in a car accident. The week after that, my new VW bus was stolen (never recovered). Two weeks after that my mother died, and the day after Christmas, my beloved grandmother had a fatal heart attack. I went under. I developed a sinus/ear/throat/wisdom tooth abcess, and when all that was finally cleared up and the tooth taken, the surgeon damaged a nerve that left part of my face without sensation, and though I could talk, there was just no possibility of singing. [Virginia is a serious student of opera.] I really thought it was gone for good.

While I was down, just before New Year's 1974, a very dear friend of my grandmother came over and loaned me the oddest-looking little box. It had a window on one side, a funny thing sticking out of the top, and all kinds of odd little dials. I twisted the dials, and pushed the switch that said "on" . . . and the <u>Enterprise</u> flew in my window. No kidding, that's really how it happened. We'd never had a TV, and I'd actually—believe it or not!—never looked at one! What I caught happened to be the first half of "The Menagerie," so of course I had to watch the second half. By then, I was hopelessly hooked! And <u>that</u> was the point at which I came back to life. In May, my sister introduced me to Shirley Maiewski [another Welcommittee worker]; in August I was in deep enough to volunteer to take over publishing "A Piece of the Action" and be trying to get in touch with Nichelle [Nichols] about running a club for her; in November 1974 I put out my first issue of P/A, and was printing the first NNFC [Nichelle Nichols Fan Club] publication for the January and February New York Cons. I may be a late bloomer, but I sure catch up fast! <u>Star Trek</u> shoved a whole new set of ideas in front of my nose. And, like the donkey and the carrot on the stick, I started moving forward again.

What continues to amaze me is the whole new person I've become. My field of interest is now virtually unlimited, whereas before I wore blinders . . . maybe I've grown up. Having the props forcibly removed tends to make one develop self-reliance! . . . When my car was stolen, it contained literally my entire past—all my clippings, programs, notes, diplomas. As I began to come alive again, I realized that I could never possess my past anyway. The only thing we ever really have is the future, and the present determines the future. My future will become whatever my present makes it. And all I can really say about my present is that every moment I am trying to make it the very best present it can be.

Are all STAR TREK fans this seriously inclined? One youngster, apparently approaching STAR TREK fandom with extreme dedication, wrote:

Being a <u>Star Trek</u> nut takes a lot of work. It means hours of article cutting, perusing book stores, stalking stores and building models.

According to Gene Roddenberry, "If there's one thing we've noticed about STAR TREK fans, whether they're six years old or eighty, they are very young-minded people. And young-minded people have an interest in the future, where we're going, what wonderful things we can achieve, and what terrible problems might face us if we don't plan for it. There's never been a time in history that I know of when youth has been confronted with so much pessimism about their own future. A kid of twelve or a man of twenty doesn't have to be a great student to recognize that inside of ten or twenty years Guatemala's going to have the H-bomb too, and Patagonia, and large cartels, and maybe wealthy private individuals. He doesn't have to be terribly well-read or have a terribly high I.Q. to see that if science continues inventing all of these things, literally hundreds of things are going to come along which can destroy us. And as a result,

STAR TREK came along and said, 'Hey, we made it!' It's a program that said there is basic intelligence and goodness and decency in the human animal that will triumph over these things.

"Now, this is a powerful message to people who are facing all of this, and I see nothing extraordinary about the fact that so many people thinking about these things said, 'Wow, STAR TREK is my baby, because it's saying what I've got to hear.' It's saying some of the things a good psychiatrist says to people to get them out of a depression."

One of STAR TREK's young-thinking fans, a middle-aged woman who earns her living as a stenographer for the State of California, writes:

```
Dear Mr. Roddenberry,
   I love Star Trek! I have watched it
since the beginning—fall of 1966, and
also the reruns. I even watch the car-
toon version in spite of kidding I re-
ceive. I have seen each episode over and
over at least eight times.
   What attracted me to Star Trek was its
action-adventure format with its central
hero character. Even at my age, Captain
Kirk is my hero . . . The fascination
this television series continues to hold
for me is it has aroused my interest in
subjects from science and technology to
mythology. For example, astronomy, U.S.
Navy, weaponry, computers, Greek myth-
ology, navigation, increase in English
vocabulary, etc.
   I am not planning on writing for TV
and do not belong to a fan club. I am
just an ardent TV viewer. I have been
watching TV for the past 23 years, and
of all the shows I have watched, Star
Trek holds the greatest fascination for
me. As creator and executive producer of
```

Star Trek, you are on my list of most-admired persons, which includes Walt Disney.

> Sincerely yours,
> Yoshiko Tamai
> Sacramento, CA

Of course, some fans are too young to remember even ten years of television, and many of the younger generation take STAR TREK at face value. One young girl wrote:

I am just beginning to like Star Trek. My cousin is teaching me everything about Star Trek. He already taught me about how the captain swears to do everything to protect his ship from danger!

What, then, is the appeal to these children, too young to need to worry about the future of our planet? Gene says the very young ones see STAR TREK as a completely different thing:

"They see it as young people see *Gulliver's Travels* —a marvelous fairy tale. You have to grow up to again read *Gulliver's Travels* and realize that Jonathan Swift wrote it as satire on the religion and the politics of his time. They see STAR TREK as good knights and black knights and damsels in distress and a marvelous fairy tale. No doubt most of the very young people—six, eight, ten years old—see STAR TREK as stories of magic and wonder. But I think even those kids are affected by the fact that STAR TREK was really a vehicle of hope and optimism."

Some of the young fans actually "live" STAR TREK. For example:

I have so many things of Star Trek, that my room is starting to look like Captain Kirk's quarters.

Apparently, today's children are not too far removed from yesterday's generation of children. There was no TV in Gene Roddenberry's childhood, but there were books and films:

"In my day, kids played Tarzan. I remember a period when I was eight or nine years old. I identified with Tarzan. At that time I was an asthmatic, and the idea of identifying with this strong lord of the jungle who could fight giant beasts for good, and do marvelously good things, appealed to me. I didn't want to live in this coughing, whooping world I was in, with the other guys on the playground hitting the ball farther than I could. I remember one afternoon when I sat up on top of the chicken coop and yodeled the Tarzan yell for about four hours on end, dreaming my own dreams. I was up there at the top of the jungle, defiantly challenging all of the evil in the world. And I think STAR TREK has some of that, too. Perhaps some of those subliminal memories were there when I wrote STAR TREK. I am a romantic. Unlike a lot of people, although I grew older, I never changed my opinion that there are, in the scheme of things, ways and guarantees that good and decency and integrity will out in the end."

Perhaps responding to this feeling, one child wrote:

```
The most valuable things in our house
are the TV which I can watch Star Trek
on and my four Star Trek books, along
with some models.
```

Then he sadly noted:

```
About a month or two ago I had a real
bad accident. I accidentally stepped on
my Enterprise, and there went the best
model in the world.
```

One interesting letter was received at STAR TREK Enterprises (now known as Lincoln Enterprises*), which expressed some of the very optimism Gene had

---
* See Appendix for address.

been speaking of. It was from a Vietnam veteran, who wrote:

> It took quite a while for Star Trek and me to get together. Back in September of 1966, when the series made its debut on NBC, I had just enlisted in the Army, and fiction, science or otherwise, was the farthest thing from my mind. After serving nine months in Vietnam, I was wounded and sent back to the States. As a result of this wound, a plate now replaces a small area of my forehead, which led to a disability retirement from the Service in May, 1968. By this time, Star Trek, as a continuing series, had been cancelled by NBC [sic] but that didn't bother me, I never knew it existed. Four more years went by, during which my opinion of mankind's future was, to say the least, very grim.
>
> It was about two years ago when Star Trek and I finally met. As coincidence would have it, the first episode I saw was "The Man Trap," which, as you know, was Star Trek's debut on September 8, 1966. I found the main characters and special effects very entertaining but the story itself was a bit too unreal for me, at that time, to consider the series anything more than fun-adventure for children. The following week, I was intrigued by the capsule given in the television listing and decided to watch again. The episode was "Errand of Mercy," and without sounding like some kind of fanatic, the greatest compliment I could give that story would be an understatement. It was as if an egotistical door of ignorance, tightly closed

in my mind, was slowly pushed open and the onrush of thousands of dreams, possibilities, probabilities and theories, all mixed with hope, knocked it right off its hinges . . .

Before closing this letter, I would like to mention that *Star Trek* has become far more than adventure stories of outer space exploration. To some, it is a dream . . . a hope of an exciting future, and to them I can only say, "Amen." As I see it, the philosophy of *Star Trek* can be applied to the present, in order to attain this goal. People should have pride in themselves and their nationality, but not to the point where this pride controls their lives. There should be an additional and greater pride, in that we are all human beings and a part of humanity, within the scheme of existence, and with this knowledge we should use all the logic, understanding and compassion we have to control our superficial fear and hatred, which alienate people from people and country from country. If there are to be starships in our future, they must be constructed by all the people, living, learning and working in harmony. Within the next two hundred and ninety-one years, or hopefully sooner, when the travelers of our planet meet whatever life there is beyond the stars, they can say with pride, "We are from the United World of Earth."

May you and all, live long and prosper.

Yours truly,
Kenneth R. Westfall
Jamaica, NY

A professor from Indian Hills Community College, Centerville, Iowa, found herself and her colleagues caught up in the mania:

Dear Sirs:

I came close to blowing up my TV set when NBC cancelled the show which has no equal. Among the literati of my acquaintance (over the past twelve years as a professor of English language and literature), <u>Star Trek</u> has always been a "must." It is endlessly absorbing to watch the development of "the beautiful crew"—Kirk, Spock, McCoy, Scotty, Uhura and Sulu. I've never seen anything quite like it, and I don't suppose I ever will again. Our hats are all off eternally to the makers of one of the genuine rarities of our era—a TV series which exhausts superlatives in its praise.

Sincerely yours,
Sherry Anne Newell

One of the most meaningful things that some STAR TREK fans feel can happen to them is to be personally issued a "Flight Deck Certificate" by none other than The Great Bird himself. Often, after appearing at a college as guest lecturer, Gene will honor his hosts with one of these deluxe eight-by-ten-inch certificates.

The reactions are astounding. For instance, many science-fiction readers will recognize Chad Oliver as a versatile author. He is also a professor of anthropology at the University of Texas. Further, he and his young son, Glen, also dig STAR TREK. Upon returning from Texas to Los Angeles following a lecture, Gene sent Glen Oliver a Flight Deck Certificate. Professor Oliver wrote the following:

Dear Gene,
I cannot thank you enough for your

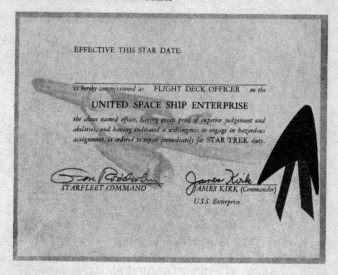

good letter and your wonderful gift for Glen. The faith of a child is a precious thing, and you have certainly restored his. He was absolutely thrilled, and figures he just has to wait a few years to sail off with the <u>Enterprise.</u> Who knows? He might make it.

                                      Regards,
                                      Chad Oliver

I might add that Dr. Oliver seems somewhat of a Trekker himself, as in a later letter he noted:

    I will now repair my <u>Enterprise</u> model (for the umpteenth time), and feed my dog (Captain James T. Kirk).

A visit to Rice University in Houston resulted in the following letter from the chairman of the Forum Committee:

Dear Mr. Roddenberry,
    I cannot tell you how exciting your

visit here was. The program was a great
success, probably the largest event held
on campus all year . . . I especially
enjoyed being made a Flight Deck Officer
of the U.S.S. Enterprise. My only question is, where do I report for duty?
                        Live long and prosper,
                        N. Wayne Hale

If you happen to have an extra twenty-five hundred dollars that you don't know what to do with, you might wish to charter *Starship I,* a private airliner owned by Los Angeles entrepreneur Howard C. Sylvester. An article about this rent-a-jet appeared in the Los Angeles *Times* and caught Gene's attention. The following correspondence was the result:

                        October 17, 1973
Dear Mr. Sylvester:
  Someone showed me the L.A. Times article on your jetliner Starship I. As an
ex-airline pilot I found it quite interesting.
  Also, I noted the comment that the
name came out of your "sentimental regard for the old television series Star
Trek" and I couldn't let this pass without sending you the enclosed Flight Deck
Certificate.
  Live long and prosper!
                        Best Regards,
                        Gene Roddenberry

                        6 November, 1973
Dear Mr. Roddenberry:
  Thank you so much for your thoughtfulness in sending me the Flight Deck Certificate, which now graces an honored

spot between Emmy and my Batman and Robin calendar.

I hope to have the pleasure of welcoming you aboard <u>Starship</u> <u>I</u>.

Yours truly,
H. C. Sylvester, Jr.

Finally, K. A. Ehricke, Executive Advisor of Space Systems and Applications at North American Rockwell, Downey, California, had these comments on his Flight Deck Certificate:

Dear Gene:

It is a great honor and privilege to be assigned to do duty on Captain Kirk's star ship. I couldn't possibly express to you how much I wished this were reality. But already the pre-reality which you created got to me emotionally more than anything since 1928. Among the many great scenes of which your series was so rich, "The Bridge" got to me more than any other because it combined technology with the disciplined and humane spirit of the crew. What greater accomplishment can there be than to achieve the wisdom through which power and knowledge can be raised from mere capabilities to values! It is this principle you kept so beautifully alive throughout the series and, to me, it somehow centered in "The Bridge."

I shall frame this memorable certificate commissioning me as Flight Deck Officer of the U.S.S. <u>Enterprise</u>.

Cordially yours,
K. A. Ehricke
North American Rockwell

The six-year-old responsible for the epigraph of

this chapter ("Wud you plees tell me wiy you tock *Star Trek* off the arr?") refused to let spelling interfere with expressing his love for STAR TREK. His letter continues:

> Why did you tack <u>Star Trek</u> off the arr. Air you going to poot <u>Star Trek</u> on the air. I like Spock and Captain Kirk and Bons and Soolo and Chekof. I like the shoe and so duse ma sistr dose to and I like it the best. I wud like to nown wiy you tock <u>Star Trek</u> of the air. Plees wud you tell me wiy you tock <u>Star Trek</u> off the arr.

Other children seem to be having a similar problem, but they manage to convey their messages. As in this one:

> . . . and since Willame Shatner is my favrat acktor will you pleas send me an antograph picture of Spok and Kik. Pleas pleas pleas.

As a former schoolteacher, my first impulse should be to grab a red pencil and start slashing corrections all over these and similar letters. But I really admire these kids for trying to express themselves, even if they do have a tendency toward creative spelling. For example, the nine-year-old who, in struggling to write about the villainous Klingons, came close, producing: "glingongs!" Here is another imaginatively spelled letter:

> Dear <u>Star Trek</u>:
> I think you probably got my first letter. I'll be written often, sorta a pinpal you might say, that is if you'll write. I've drawn some pitchers for ya. Hope ya don't mind my slang. I've goten

"Yoleman Janess" and unidentified crewmember.

a new Star Trek model, the Enterprise.
I've painted the window some yellow some
black, I've painted the engenes and em-
pulse engenes and everything else that
was soposed to be painted the right
color! How do you like m pitcher? I love
monsters, and aspectaley Star Trek, I've
got a big Drackela poster on my wall,
and a lot of Star Trek pictures. I'm
going to be Mr. Spock, Capt. Kirk, or
Scotty on Holloween.
P.S. I love Yoleman Janess.

If the children seem stricken with STAR TREK*mania,* here is an example of a parent who loved the show so much that he named a child after an episode title:

Dear Sir or Miss:
Many things have been taken from the
TV show Star Trek, and I am notifying
you of another.
The birth certificate copy I am sending along is to show you that we have
named our daughter after the Star Trek
episode "Miri." I do not know if we are
the first or not, it truly would be interesting to know . . .
We thought the name a most beautiful
one, so we decided to use it. We knew
there would be some hassle with people
pronouncing it or even spelling it correctly, but little did we know how much
of a hassle. Many spell it "Mary," or
"Miry," or "Mari," or any other form of
the name. Pronouncing it is altogether
another story. Nonetheless we still like
it and think it is a beautiful name, and
even perhaps one to catch on in the
future.
Thank you for your time and trouble. I

hope you enjoyed learning this little bit of information, as I always do about the program <u>Star Trek</u>. It will live forever.

> Sincerely yours,
> Richard E. Elliott
> Redwood City, CA

The birth certificate enclosed with the letter shows that Miri Suzanne Elliott made her debut in San Mateo County, California, on May 19, 1974. May she live long and prosper!

One set of parents even refused to allow their child to be born until after a STAR TREK episode was completed.

Dear *Star Trek* Productions:

My husband and I have been avid fans of *Star Trek* ever since it was started. We even watched it when we were stationed in England for three years. We have seen each episode so many times I couldn't even count them.

I had to write and tell you of a particular incident that happened a couple of years ago. I was expecting our first baby and had started into labor in the mid-afternoon. I telephoned my husband at work and asked him to come home and drive me to the hospital. He arrived just as *Star Trek* began. We decided that we couldn't miss it so we sat for one hour timing my contractions and watching *Star Trek.* (The contractions were 5-7 minutes apart by then.) Well, I made it to the hospital in plenty of time to give birth to our little boy and see *Star Trek*, too.

                Sincerely,
                Mrs. Edward V. Sedgwick, III
        Pass Christian, MS

With STAR TREK*mania* showing no signs of abating, we were quite fortunate to have the STAR TREK Welcommittee organized by Helen Young of Houston, Texas. STAR TREK Welcommittee is a nonprofit service organization (not a club to join) with 140 volunteer workers in 35 states who devote their time and effort to answering questions about STAR TREK, at no charge, and with the STAR TREK office's undying gratitude, I might add. (For complete information on the Welcommittee, see the Appendix.) It is people like the Welcommittee volunteers who have added impetus to the STAR TREK snowball rolling across this country and others throughout the world, collecting people and ideas and leaving in its path a wake of hunger and thirst for more. Is there some way perhaps to harness this energy generated by the millions of STAR TREK followers? Gene Roddenberry had one final thought on that:

"Having become aware that there are many people out there who are interested in the STAR TREK philosophy and the ideas we tried to propagate on the show (and I think they were good ideas—decency and tolerance and love and all of those things), I wonder if there isn't some way to turn their interest to some greater good. Perhaps to write something in which all the ideas were laid out as a philosophy, a way of life that would *give* direction to those seeking guidelines, and which would articulate all of the positive values STAR TREK tried to demonstrate in a way that would be meaningful and helpful. People have mentioned that this pool of well-motivated viewers is too valuable a resource, too exciting a reservoir of interest and hunger, for ideas and ideals to just go to waste."

D. C. Fontana (left) and Helen Young at the New York Convention (February 1973). Photo by Dr. Lum P. Fischer.

Chapter Two

The Universal Appeal

```
Is Lieutenant O'Hura Irish?
            —Secretary at
              Harvard University
```

I

A black female lieutenant. An Oriental helmsman. A Russian ensign. A Southern WASP doctor. A Scottish engineer. An alien of Vulcan-Earth parentage, with pointed ears and green blood.

Ingredients for a television show or a recipe for civil war? The odds would seem to favor the second choice, but anyone who has ever watched STAR TREK knows that the above characters work together in a cohesive group, and almost no one seems aware of any racial, religious, or cultural differences. Even television of the middle 1970s would be hard-pressed to find a more varied yet homogeneous group, reaching in syndication audiences in 150 cities of the United States and over 60 foreign nations!

Why does STAR TREK have such wide appeal? Gene Roddenberry, the creator of this mini-United Nations in space, explained it this way:

"I think STAR TREK was a first in television, having a mixed, international crew of various colors and ideas and cultures and philosophies. It just seemed to me most implicitly obvious that if mankind makes it into the next century, all of those things that have divided us—color, race, religion, culture, and so on—can no longer divide us. Petty nationalism has got to go. We will not make it unless we have begun to cherish the differences between people, instead of being afraid of them. I think variety gives life a lovely quality: Irishmen and Jews and blacks and Asians, all bring a fascinating kaleidoscope of wonderful things. It just seemed obvious to me that that's what we at STAR TREK had to do.

"In 1964 I was faced with the fact that there were not a lot of different races on TV. I don't know if it was so much a network practice as it was an historical accident. We could have been much better on STAR TREK: I wanted the ship to be something like half men and half women; I would have loved, instead of having Captain Kirk obviously American, to have had him English or Italian or South American; I would have liked to have had Scotty, Bones, and the 'in-group' not all Caucasian Protestant types. But in 1964–65, when we were putting it all together, I was playing to an audience that was demanding the WASP image. I had to curb my attitudes and present a group of actors that the network would accept and a mass audience would accept, and then, during the show, bring in others. You've probably noticed in some episodes that when they would talk to other ships, a woman or perhaps a Latin would be a captain. Even *that* we didn't do as much as we would have liked, because, again, you can push an audience only so far. You have to infiltrate new ideas subtly. Many times a character was written with no description, and Joe D'Agosta, our casting man, and Gene Coon* would bring in a black and say, 'I think he's the man for the part.' And he wouldn't be brought in because he was black, but because he was a good actor who could play the part."

Gene is a man with a great love for all people, and it was only natural that this would be incorporated into the STAR TREK "philosophy." Apparently such a philosophy does have its threads woven throughout the series, as aware viewers have written many interesting letters on the ideas and ideals STAR TREK expressed. Sandra Morse of West Jordan, Utah, writes:

> The outstanding theme of Star Trek seemed to be that man would eventually conquer the meanness and smallness of today, and be able to intelligently co-exist with other life forms. If man's mind could conceive of such a time, then

---

* The late Gene Coon was line producer of STAR TREK for two seasons.

eventually man will accomplish such a goal.

More and more do we need shows such as *Star Trek*, especially in these days of ever increasing anarchy. Above all, we need *Star Trek* to show us that there *is* hope for mankind.

Barbara Moss of El Centro, California, found personal satisfaction in this hope for the future:

For me *Star Trek* was something very special. It helped me realize that there are some good people out there. There was a time back in 1971 when I thought life wasn't worth living. I was always warned of all the bad things going on in the world. (There's too much crime, there's too much hate, the racial discrimination, etc.) I was never told of the good things that were happening.

Unfortunately, I had a tendency to believe everything I heard. Until I found *Star Trek*, and after a few months of watching it, I began to realize that the world is not just a big bundle of hate. I saw all the love in *Star Trek*. They didn't live in a world of prejudices, and I thought, well maybe, just maybe a lot of what I had heard was exaggerated a bit, so I decided I would stop listening to all the talk and find out for myself. And I found I was right. People can and do work and live well together, if they want to. I realized something else too. There is still a lot of crime and hate and racial discrimination in the world, and there will be until someone does something to change it. And it's going to have to be the younger generations who make that change. Only we're not going to if we give it all up. Star Trek showed me that. In a way, Star Trek kind of saved my life.

Sincerely,
Barbara Moss

A Wisconsin nurse writes:

The mutual cooperation and the social harmonies among a crew of different races, creeds and planetary origins (as was that of the Enterprise) sets the scene for looking at our own prejudices, social indifferences, and intolerances. How silly to feel threatened by our own differences of color, philosophy, and social standing when co-existence is an alternative within our reach. Through your show you told the world that the differences among ourselves can be stimulating, exciting, interesting and informative . . . Star Trek was one of the few shows that assumed its audience wasn't composed of idiots. I found that very refreshing . . . When this nurse was a poor, struggling, highly pressured student, Star Trek brought me much enjoyment and release of tension. For that I am eternally grateful.

Live long and prosper,
Diana Pasch

A nun, teaching at Oregon State University, wrote a letter which has become one of Gene's most treasured:

8 July, 1974

Dear Mr. Roddenberry:

Although it may seem rather late in time for this, I thought I would write to you to tell you how much I like Star

Trek, and since you are its originator, to say thank you. Portland's independent TV station just began re-running the re-runs after several months without them, and it occurred to me, as I was watching one of the episodes, that any TV show that can generate the same delight the fifth or sixth time around must really be something extraordinary. I really haven't seen the whole series that often, in fact there are some that I am still waiting to see for the first time. Originally, I missed most of the first and about half of the second year due to the exigencies of the monastic horarium (I am a Benedictine nun) so I am dependent on the whims of the program director of Channel 12 right now to catch up. Given the random sequence in which the episodes are shown, and the rather high frequency with which they are pre-empted for more "significant programming"—like Canadian football games—I figure it's going to take me about five more years to see them all, if we both last that long. It's something to look forward to, though.

In case you are interested in my credentials, besides being a member of the Order of St. Benedict, I have two degrees in chemistry and am currently on leave from my college faculty appointment to finish my PhD in nuclear radiation chemistry and other things here at O.S.U. Most of my friends consider my affection for Star Trek as a kind of weakness of mind, or character, or both, and I must confess I agree with them sometimes, because when it comes down to the basics, it's not really great art, or great literature or great drama—if you'll pardon my saying so, some of the plots are even kind of silly. As far as I can determine, its essential charm lies in the fact that it embodies a self-consistent subsidiary world that has achieved a sort of reality of its own that can endure as good-in-itself in spite of the deficiencies of plot or style. It's as though the world of the _Enterprise_ were an image which recalls to mind our intuitive knowledge of some Platonic reality. Maybe that isn't such a metaphysical fancy after all. You may already have seen the attached essay by Andrew Greeley (a sociologist from Chicago). What he says is, I think, quite true. _Star Trek_ is one of the very few television programs that deal with the ethical/moral issues (even though only implicitly) which some of us feel to be the basic and most important issues that man can confront. Therefore, it _is_ an image of the realest of all worlds.

I'm afraid I might be getting carried away in assigning such a solemn significance to an ephemeral thing whose chief object is entertainment. Maybe I'm just trying to rationalize my own weakness of mind—I hope not! A few years ago, though, I ran across a passage in Christopher Fry's verse play "A Sleep of Prisoners," and was delighted by the last lines. The play on words, although entirely unintentional, is, I think, so appropriate to what I have been saying:

This is no winter now; the frozen misery of centuries breaks, cracks, begins to
  move;

the thunder is the thunder of the floes,
the thaw, the flood, the upstart spring.
Thank God our time is <u>now</u>, when wrong
comes up to face us everywhere,
never to leave us till we take
the longest stride of soul men ever
  took.
Affairs are now soul size.
The enterprise
is exploration into God.

    That's a great line to end this on, but I still have a couple of things to say. I have seen a few of the Saturday morning animated *Star Trek* programs, and find them, of course, lacking. The medium is so severely limited that it can produce only caricatures of the original. I can say for it, that as a kid program, it is vastly superior to the other animated kid programs; however, I am sorry to see *Star Trek* become at last what its critics always wrongly accused it of being.

    I have a dim recollection of seeing two TV movies with which I believe you were associated: one of which I liked. (I hope that <u>was</u> your movie, I will be embarrassed if I'm wrong.) The android was, of course, another incarnation of Spock. It's rather ironic, isn't it, that the characters who speak most significantly to the human condition should be non-human.

    You are no doubt trying for another series that will take *Star Trek*'s place. I am sorry to say that I don't think you will be able to do it. We who love the original are never going to be able to accept imitations!

I hope that somewhere in this rather disconnected ramble I have <u>said</u> something. My best wishes for whatever enterprise may now be your concern.

    Sincerely,
    Sister Margaret J. Clarke, O.S.B.

○

August 14, 1974

Dear Sister Clarke:

Thank you for the verse from Christopher Fry's <u>A Sleep of Prisoners</u>. I had never seen it and am delighted to find something which so perfectly expresses something I have long felt. The challenges of mankind, indeed, now become soul-size and we will survive only if we merit survival by meeting the world's problems with soul-sized solutions.

It is a pleasure to receive a letter from someone who . . . puts the show into its proper perspective. I am also happy to find that some people do understand that <u>Star Trek</u> was, within the limits and requirements of mass audience television, an attempt to express something of my own philosophy. I use that term at the risk of seeming to dignify what were actually rather simplistic observations, but comment is, after all, the obligation of the writer in whatever medium he works.

The problem faced by the television writer is that the networks have an almost pathological fear of any comment on any meaningful subject. For them, television exists for the single purpose of attracting as many potential product purchasers as possible and holding them there from commercial to commercial. Its sole purpose is to sell beer, spray deodorant, soap, and so on. They are not interested in attracting people who think too deeply (since they are not likely to be influenced by the commercials) and neither do they want their mass audience distracted by too much thinking in the intervals between commercial messages. Their ideal program would be one which manages to attract and hold that audience while keeping the quality of its content just low enough to make the commercials seem, by comparison, to be bright and sparkling moments. Of course, most good writers try constantly to subvert this process by disguising their comments and making them so integral to the plot line that the network representative on the show can demand their exclusion only at the risk of destroying the audience-attracting entertainment values.

Many of us writers become producers because it considerably expands our opportunities to infiltrate our own comments into programs. We can suggest ideas to writers who are working for us and, failing there, either rewrite or polish the script so that comments are included. Also, as the creative head of the show (unlike the producer in motion pictures), the television producer can guarantee that the week-to-week comments in the series maintain some kind of philosophical continuity. It is sometimes possible to shape the format and the characters of a new series so that there is not only more opportunity for (disguised) comment, but it even becomes necessary in order to maintain the characterizations and the format.

Star Trek, of course, was a Jonathan Swift approach to this whole problem. It occurred to me that network executives would view alien planets and life forms and even our futuristic ship and crew as so unreal that our comments would not be recognized as anything really pertinent to today. After all, why worry about what some little polka-dotted life form on Polaris IX thinks about war, religion, procreation, economics, and so on? And they also felt no need to be concerned about what was being said in the many stories which were, as you correctly point out, rather silly in nature.

Few TV pilots manage to do this and still get on the air as a series. The Questor Tapes was an example of a program which was actually purchased by NBC but failed to get on the air because I refused to make certain changes on the comment-provoking aspects of the character and the format. They wanted it to become a robot, Superman show which would draw its entertainment from Questor's ability to leap tall buildings in a single bound, or something like that. They insisted on entirely deleting the back story of The Questor Tapes, more particularly Questor's mission to help mankind and his computer-logic perspectives on mankind by which the weekly episodes would have aimed at seeing ourselves as others might see us.

Incidentally, I also agree with your comment that Star Trek was not really great literature or great drama. It seems to me, however, it might merit some consideration as art since art must be judged in context with its medium. A man who produces temporary things with colored sand on a London sidewalk is not necessarily less an artist than one who creates in finer detail and perspective through the advantages of oils and canvas. Considering the limitations imposed by television time and budget (the equivalent of making half a motion picture every week), and the absolute requirement of using common denominators capable of attracting a mass audience minimum of around 18 million viewers, I think the impact of *Star Trek* suggests a rather artistic use of the few colored sands at our disposal.

Forgive my going into some detail on the above. These are thoughts I have been meaning to write into a lecture series I am giving this fall at various universities. My pleasure and interest in your letter created an opportunity to get some of it down on paper. I hope to meet you some day and will certainly make it a point to do so if I am ever scheduled to give a talk in your area. For some reason, college *Star Trek* fans seem to want to see and hear me, and I get the double return advantage of deriving some income from it while keeping abreast of what is happening and how people are thinking in places other than the television communities in Hollywood and New York. It seems to me that young people today are remarkable humans and a writer can derive a great deal from the stimulation in meeting and hearing from them.

THE UNIVERSAL APPEAL 45

I'm glad you wrote.

                    Best wishes,
                    Gene Roddenberry

II

A tree grows in Israel. It was planted by Daniel Guttman of Minneapolis in February, 1974, in honor of Gene Roddenberry. Daniel writes:

Dear Mr. Roddenberry,
When I started to write this letter

within the confines of my head, I tried not to sound too much like an irrational fan, but I found it too hard to disguise the fact.

I am, as you can see from the letterhead, Dan Guttman. I am currently 15 years old and have been a fan of both Star Trek and N.A.S.A. for much of my life . . . I do have a deep-rooted interest in both Star Trek and you. Star Trek, because of my interest in space exploration, life on other planets, and especially science fiction; you because I like to consider myself a writer . . .

Now to explain the enclosed. I have made it my tradition to plant a tree in honor of an astronaut in Israel every year on the Jewish holiday of Tu Bishvat. This year I decided to plant a tree in honor of a creator of astronauts. Now there stands a tree in Israel planted in honor of the man who wrote Genesis II, the magnificent Questor, and the one-of-a-kind Star Trek . . . Star Trek is one of the most livable shows ever produced. Every time I watch it, I feel that I, too, am on the Enterprise.

                Sincerely yours,
                Daniel Isaac Guttman

STAR TREK's appeal to members of many different religious and ethnic groups is another aspect of the universal appeal. Christine V. Kemp, a member of the American Baptist Board of Education and Publication, in association with American Baptist Churches USA, writes:

                November 10, 1972
Dear Mr. Roddenberry:
After months of discussion with

American Baptist staff, we have decided to ask you to consider producing a second five-year mission for the starship Enterprise.

The original Star Trek program was a masterpiece. The combination of religious message, character interaction, and human response to crisis made the program a true public service as well as excellent entertainment.

I believe the time is ripe for a second series. The original now in syndication has a large and loyal following. With advance publicity, the show could be exceptionally successful. The religious community could be a solid backer of the show, as it would be excellent for discussion starters, small groups and church schools.

If I can be of any help, please let me know.

Cordially yours,
Christine V. Kemp
Valley Forge, PA

Another religious group wrote to request the use of the film "Who Mourns for Adonais." While we had to deny this request, due to studio policy, we were curious as to how the religious school felt this would benefit their teachings. Here is their reply:

October 17, 1975

Ours is a humanistic Jewish congregation, and all materials that our teachers are familiar with are considered for use in our school. Our sixth-grade teacher, Lee Prince, is a Star Trek devotee. His response to your letter is as follows:

". . . Star Trek as a series was particularly effective in communicating to children. We were working on the Creation story in the Bible, and other mythological interpretations of creation, in addition to man's subsequent learning from the tree of good and evil of life.

" 'Who Mourns for Adonais' first puts the students into a frame of mind where they are prepared to accept an extraterrestrial being who chooses to call himself a god. As the god shows himself more arbitrary, the crew of the Enterprise is forced to destroy it ('learning good and evil'). But there is regret unto the very end in the story. After all, one of the crew members had fallen in love with the god and believed he might return them to a state of nature (Garden of Eden?). And even Captain Kirk is forced at the end to voice something on the order of 'Would it hurt us, I wonder, to gather a few laurel leaves?' All these themes and subthemes in one episode! Of course, 'The Apple' dealt more specifically with a Garden of Eden setting and we did read from the Blish adaptation from it, but 'Who Mourns for Adonais' was 1) more exciting and 2) dealt with the themes we wanted our students to consider."

Sincerely,
Margery Buxbaum
Director of Religious Education
Congregation Beth Or
Deerfield, IL

In 1974, Gene received a letter from the Armenian Students' Association of America, requesting his com-

THE UNIVERSAL APPEAL 49

ments on a passage in the STAR TREK episode "Errand of Mercy." The letter says:

> In this episode Capt. Kirk, in summarizing the plight of the Organians to Mr. Spock, says ". . . another Armenia, always the innocents in the paths of the invasion routes."
>
> We would like to know how you feel about Armenians, and how this memory of the Armenians' plight has survived to Captain Kirk's time (the 23rd century). Any response by you on the above quoted statement and/or personal remarks would be greatly appreciated.
>
> Thank you,
> William Hovespian
> Upper Darby, PA

Gene replied:

> Regarding the Star Trek episode entitled "Errand of Mercy," this was written by Gene L. Coon, a dear friend now deceased, who was also producer of Star Trek when I moved to executive producer. He was well acquainted with the history of the Armenians and I remember we had a long talk about it once at the time he learned I had been in an airplane crash in the vicinity of Deir Ez Zor,* Syria. I'm sure any Armenian student knows why this name caught his attention.
>
> As for myself, the history of my interest in the Armenian people began early. When I began writing in television, I used some of my small knowledge

---

* Deir Ez Zor marked the end of the death march the Turks forced the Armenians on in the early 1900s.

of the people and culture to write a <u>Have</u> <u>Gun</u> <u>Will</u> <u>Travel</u> script entitled "Helen of Apiginian," which won me my first national writing award. It was not a particularly deep treatment, concerning the plight of a young cowboy who was thought to have kidnapped a lovely Armenian girl. In the end, it turns out to be more a kidnapping by this lovely but exceptionally warm-blooded young female. The principal character in the piece was her father, a man of enormous personality and drawn somewhat on the lines of a Saroyan "Uncle" which I particularly liked. In it, I used the series hero, Paladin, to echo some of my own warm sentiments about the Armenian personality, dishes, customs, and so on.

All this despite the fact that an Armenian usually hurts me a couple of times each year. My dentist.

Sincerely yours,
Gene Roddenberry

During the summer of 1975, when Gene had begun working on a first draft of a script for possible use in the projected STAR TREK motion picture, I teasingly chided him for not having any Jewish names among all the other minorities on board the *Enterprise* (ignoring the fact that the actors playing Captain Kirk, Mr. Spock, and Ensign Chekov are Jewish). As a joke, I sent Gene the following memo:

To: Gene "Roddenberry"
From: Susan "Sakovsky"
    Date: July 28, 1975
    Subject: The Yiddish Connection

After many hours of dedicated research (recalling names of past acquaintances and reading the Burbank phone book),

THE UNIVERSAL APPEAL 51

I have compiled a list of "typically Jewish" surnames. Bearing in mind that there is no such thing as a typically Jewish surname, the following list may, of course, be ignored, since everyone knows that anyone with any of these names would immediately have it changed to "Smith" or "Jones" or possibly "Roddenberry" (e.g., Roddenberg, Roddenstein, Roddenowitz or Roddensky):

>   Abrams   Jacobson
>   Blum   Kaufman
>   Cohen   Kaplin
>   Eisenberg   Koplowitz
>   Epstein   Koppelman
>   Feinstein   Levine
>   Feldman   Levy
>   Goldberg   Lipschitz
>   Goldstein   Marx
>   Hirshfeld   Nussbaum
>   Horowitz   Perlman
>   Israel   Perlmutter
>   Rosenstein
>   " feld
>   " blatt, etc.
>   Rosoff
>   Schwartz
>   Steinberg
>   Tishman
>   Weinstein
>   Weiss
>   Zemsky

Should any of the above names be selected for a crew member aboard the <u>Enterprise</u>, you might wish to consider one or more of the following typically Jewish first names (obviously you can't call them "Christian" names): Alan,

Isadore (Izzy), Joel, Sam, Mark, Max, David, Michael, Ira, Paul, Lenny, Isaac, Jacob, Abraham, Murray, Aaron, Ezra, Saul, Steve and Lou. Females, of course, are usually called "Susan." Occasionally there is a Ruth or Esther or Sarah, but rarely does this vary.

The next morning's rough-draft script dictation contained a transporter operator named Abrams. Now, if we can only get Blum through Zemsky on board!

III

Can you tell me why almost all the aliens from different planets speak English?

Obviously, most of the audience would not understand them if they spoke Aldebaranese! In Germany, where STAR TREK is aired as RAUMSCHIFF ENTERPRISE, everyone, including Captain Kirk, speaks flawless German. In Japan, Mr. Spock's "fascinating" gives way to "ah-so." In fact, the *Enterprise* has orbited over sixty countries and dependencies of one sort or another outside the United States. They are: Abu Dhabi; Argentina; Aruba; Australia; Bangladesh; Barbados; Belgium; Bermuda; Brazil; Canada; Chile; Colombia; Costa Rica; Dominican Republic; Dubai; Ecuador; El Salvador; Ethiopia; Finland; Gibraltar; Great Britain; Greece; Guatemala; Honduras; Hong Kong; Indonesia; Iran; Iraq; Ireland; Jamaica; Japan; Jordan; Kenya; Korea; Kuwait; Lebanon; Luxembourg; Malaysia; Malta; Mauritius; Mexico; Monaco; Netherlands; Nicaragua; Nigeria; Norway; Pakistan; Panama; Peru; Philippines; Qatar; Republic of China (Taiwan); Rhodesia; Sierre Leone; Singapore; Spain; South Africa; Thailand; Trinidad and Tobago; Turkey; Uganda; Venezuela; West Germany; Yugoslavia; Zambia.

THE UNIVERSAL APPEAL 53

The majority of the foreign mail STAR TREK receives is from Canada. George Gerhardt of *The Victorian Weekly,* British Columbia's largest weekly newspaper, wrote the following letter on behalf of Canadian fans:

June 5, 1972

Dear Mr. Roddenberry:

The other day a lady walked into my office with a "beef"—she wanted to know why I wasn't doing something about getting Star Trek back onto the air. I was flabbergasted.

However, after talking to her, I discovered there's a larger group of Star Trek fanatics in Canada than I really imagined. I suppose I should add that I too am an avid viewer.

My own feelings are that the cast of this show was *not* its strongest element, but the stories were practically everything. I know Bill Shatner from my days as a dresser at the Stratford Shakespearean Festival in Ontario, and consider him a most adept actor.

My readers would really like to know if there are any plans for a return of Star Trek and, if not as a series, what are the possibilities of a made-for-television movie of Star Trek each season?

I believe we'd take almost anything to get more of those terrific stories.

        Yours truly,
        George Gerhardt
        Art Director,
        The Victorian (B.C.) Weekly

The next heaviest influx of fan mail from other countries is from England and Australia. One young English fan had a truly original way of getting his letter all the way across the Atlantic, and the entire North American continent, addressing it as follows:

The 3″ × 6″ envelope was delivered by our studio mailperson, who never batted an eye.

Another young English viewer wondered if Bill Shatner knew *millions* of film stars, and if he did, could he get her their autographs? And many of our British friends just write telling us how much they enjoy the "programme" broadcast on the BBC. These are truly a delight to read, especially because nearly all of them are so legible! I think the British school systems must have had my poor eyes in mind when teaching penmanship. Also, I've found that letter writers from England and Australia tend to be a bit more formal and polite than their American counterparts. Many letters we receive from the United Kingdom are signed "Yours faithfully" followed by the name, and if it's a single female, the word "Miss" always appears parenthetically. We have yet to receive a letter from a British Ms.

One very lovely letter which Gene especially enjoyed was from an Australian family, the Woodcocks:

February 14, 1974

Dear Mr. Roddenberry,

Our sincere thanks and admiration for your creation of <u>Star Trek</u>. What an achievement, to have these wonderful characters to your credit. They are a continual delight with their genuine and honest affection, true humour and marvellous complex natures.

We managed to have a short season (only seven) of replays and it really hurts to not be able to understand why this, the most ———— (no word adequate) programme in a world of violence, is not aired with pride and great joy.

Sir, for all the hope and happiness you spread in such a short time, we wish you, Mr. Shatner, Mr. Nimoy, Mr. Kelley, Doohan, Takei, Koenig etc. etc. peace, a calm spirit, satisfaction in all you attempt, and most of all, because we are selfish, a return of our beloved crew and the gallant ship <u>Enterprise</u>.

How we long for the sight of all these old friends. William Shatner, surely he can express with his face what others would need volumes to convey. Fortunately one of the repeats was the episode "Operation Annihilate" and his one word "Bones," ground out, over Spock's blindness, made our skin actually prickle and break out into a sweat.

Leonard Nimoy—our affection for him is unbounded, as for Shatner and the rest.

How we hope some miracle will occur, and the universal message from <u>Star Trek</u> will again speak to the millions of Earthbound who can only stand and gaze at the stars.

May God bless you all,
The Woodcock Family
Inglewood, Perth
West Australia

P.S. It is quite true, too, that the sense of loss does amount to a real physical pain, and I suppose wishing is rather like empty bells ringing in empty skies. But at least we had a glimpse and an echo.

○

April 2, 1974

Dear Woodcocks,

Thanks for a kind and moving letter. When next I see Bill Shatner, Leonard Nimoy and the others, I will tell them that we have a family of extraordinary fans in West Australia and will pass on your best wishes to them.

We made seventy-nine shows in all and I do hope you get to see more of them, as they covered quite a range of ideas and experiences. But however the adventures varied, we always remained true to our basic beliefs about the dignity of life forms, the fact that no one has the right to interfere in the evolution of others, and that to be different is not necessarily to be ugly or evil.

I have never received a <u>Star Trek</u> letter which touched me more than yours, and it is precisely this kind of thing that made all the hard labor worthwhile.

Sincerely yours,
Gene Roddenberry

A young lady from Japan had these interesting things to say about STAR TREK's run on Japanese television:

<u>Star Trek</u> is popular among the young. For the present, however, Japan is far

behind America. Maybe I, too. But I want more chance to know everything concerning <u>Star Trek</u> and Spock. I am glad if you enlighten me about <u>Star Trek</u> Conventions, Trekkies and Trekism etc. through correspondence.

In last October, I saw <u>Star Trek</u> for the first time. Then <u>Star Trek</u> was rebroadcasted four times a week from Monday to Thursday in midnight. And when that broadcasting got through in this February, there was a tremendous audience response to <u>Star Trek</u>. So Kansai TV station is rebroadcasting <u>Star Trek</u> again once a week on Sunday noon. And it is expected to run for one and half year to come. What is interesting is that <u>Star Trek</u> become more popular the present rebroadcasting than first broadcasting (few years ago).

Shall I send you a cassette tape? Spock, Kirk, McCoy—they speak Japanese very well. As for me, I like Spock's Japanese voice . . . If you hear it, you must think so too.* When you listen to my cassette, I hope you can recognize each actor's voice. Zulu (is this spell correct?) is called Mr. Kato in Japan, also Scotty is Charley. Without knowing why they are called like that. Much to my regret, I do not know Spock's true voice. Therefore, I want to get it by all means.

So long and sayonara.

Sincerely yours.
Yoshiko Hirihara
Kyoto, Japan

---

* I listened to the tape, and, though I don't understand Japanese, the actor doing Mr. Spock sounded quite a bit like him.

P.S. It may sound funny, how do you pronounce Leonard? Is the "o" in Leonard not pronounced?

From the letter it was clear that Yoshiko was making good use of her Japanese-English dictionary. Original wording of this and of other foreign-language letters is used here because it preserves the flavor and zest of the letters. Obviously Yoshiko tried very hard to use correct English, and she should be quite proud of this letter.

A fan-club leader in Japan supplied the Japanese characters for STAR TREK:

宇宙大作戦

宇宙大作戦

宇宙大作戦

Two very interesting letters from Brazil showed the same enthusiasm for STAR TREK:

Dear Sirs:
I'm Brazilian and I don't know to write English very well, but I have a very good dictionary and I do the utmost for to write right.

I have a mania for scientific fiction, and I must admit that I'm very much surprised when I watch the spectacular series Star Trek.

I like very much Mr. Spock or Leonard Nimoy, and I'd like to get some posters, photographys or somethings about his life.

I thank you for your kind attention.
I subscribe respectfully,
Adriana Kfoury Pereira
Rinas Guais, Brazil

O

Dearest Gene,

My name's Sandra Berlinski. I am fourteen years old. I admire your work too much! Especially in the wonderful film that you were the creator and producer of, Star Trek.

I don't understand how you had the magnific imagination to wonder so fantastic series about space that I love so much. Gene, how did surge the wonderful idea of Star Trek? And how did you had the brilliant imagination to put a Vulcan or half Vulcan aboard the Enterprise?

The cast that was chosen is of the best quality and I think they acted Star Trek with so naturality that they looked like that they were really aboard of the U.S.S. Enterprise . . . A new series is on the way with all the original Trekkies. Isn't truth? Please, please tell me about it, all you know! You might be a wonderful person, to create Star Trek and rebegin it . . . And we fanatic Trekkies are waiting our Captain

James T. Kirk to convoke all his crew
members of the <u>Enterprise</u> and I am sure
that the Captain will give this order
with so happiness as the rest of the
crew, and we much more.

Gene, congratulations is so few to
you, you gave me fascinating moments.
And my great wish is to correspond with
so fanciful and interesting person in
this world.

                Sandra Berlinski
                Rio de Janeiro, Brazil

A very unusual request came from the friend of a small foreign-born boy learning to speak English by watching STAR TREK in his new American homeland:

Gentlemen:
On behalf of an eight-year-old boy
from Lebanon, may I ask for an autographed picture of Mr. Spock from your
<u>Star Trek</u> TV program. He is learning En-
glish from this program, and is utterly
engrossed. His first name is Habib.

                Many thanks,
                Mrs. Ruth Knight

Although we normally aren't able to secure autographed pictures, we made a special effort in this case. A thank-you note from Mrs. Knight reads:

Many thanks for the photographs, especially the one with the ears and the
lovely signature and message ["Live
Long and Prosper"]. Eight-year-old Habib
goes to a French school in New York,
talks Arabic with his mother in the
afternoons, and is glued to <u>Star Trek</u>
from 6:00 P.M. to 7:00 P.M. His father
must wait (and does) to play and talk
with his boy.

IV

If STAR TREK seemed to be concerned with fair treatment of all races, creeds, religions, nationalities, and so on, what about its treatment of women—who, incidentally, are statistically in the majority in this world?

In his original plans for STAR TREK, Gene wanted the ratio of men and women to be fifty-fifty. "They told me, you can't have that. It will look like there's a lot of fooling around going on up there in space. So we compromised and decided on 30 percent women. I figured 30 percent healthy women could handle the rest of the crew!"

"In the original pilot we had a woman as second-in-command of the *Enterprise* ('Number One,' played by Majel Barrett). The networks said they would like two major changes in the second pilot: get rid of the woman, because they felt an audience wouldn't believe a woman in any position of command; and also get rid of 'the guy with the ears,' because an audience couldn't possibly identify with an alien. I figured I could save *one,* so I kept Mr. Spock, moved him up to second-in-command, and gave him the woman's logical qualities— And I married the woman, because to do it the other way around would have been illegal in California!"

A STAR TREK fan from New Jersey wrote the following letter asking for Gene's stand on women's liberation and STAR TREK:

September 30, 1975

Dear Gene,
I would like to mention several aspects of Star Trek which I hope you will consider changing in the script(s) you are preparing. Each of these aspects contributes to a view of the women of

the future in a way I believe is unsupportable and irresponsible.

That women were viewed in this way in 1966 or 1968 is generally true, but times are changing quickly, and I cannot imagine women in 200 years accepting the costumes, hairdos, or treatment required of them in Star Trek. Furthermore, it would not be socially responsible to perpetuate such unparallel treatment of the sexes in a portrayal of a future which we hope to be less discriminatory and concerned primarily with each individual's best contribution to the combined welfare of humanity.

The costumes and make-up of women on Star Trek episodes are not realistic. Even today women generally wear clothes applicable to their jobs. To suppose that they will wear dresses, let alone skirts so short that their crotches are but inches from view, is silly. It may be what male viewers wish to see, but if so, why not have tight crotch pads or similar short skirts for the men, to cater to female fantasies? Wouldn't seem businesslike for the men, would it? The costumes in the episode "Where No Man Has Gone Before" were reasonable and dignified for both sexes. Why not use them for future scripts?

The depiction of women in the scripts is rather distasteful too. They are consistently shown in soft lights, sexy hairdos, and in scenes guaranteed to draw attention to their physical attractiveness for the men of the crew and in the audience. Again, why only the women? What this unequal treatment does is to point out to all the female viewers that it's not going to be any different, we are still going to be the sex objects, and even our professional standing will be secondary to our physical appearance and our contributions to the lives of the men around us. Not so for the men, who will contribute on the basis of their intellectual achievement. Men are Captain, Science Officer, and so on, career people first. Women are women, and oh yes, professionals until they settle down somewhere as wives and mothers. Is this really likely for the future? (It's not even so common today!)

Finally, the language used to refer to the women and men. Why the use of "girl" but not "boy" to refer to crew members? And "yeoman" for a female? How about "Where No <u>Man</u> Has Gone Before?" (In our house, the standing joke is: "Virgin space, eh?")

The most effective means I can suggest to help you understand how such treatment of women comes across is to try to imagine it all in reverse. For example:

> Male yeowoman has collapsed on the bridge. Captain (a woman, of course) orders the doctor (a woman) to "take the boy to sick bay." Boy enters the bridge. Close up, soft lights, romantic music, emphasis on the tight, sexy costume. Captain sighs, looks at the doctor, who winks at her. Boy is specialist in geophysics. Captain wonders what he'd be like in bed.

Every male guest star is the object of at least minor allusion to his sex. Emphasis for female guest stars is on their professional ability, and the plot usually centers around some dramatic action of theirs.

Landing party is in trouble. The lone male member looks pleadingly at the Captain. "I'm frightened," he says.

It's not very pleasant to see one's sex portrayed as weaker and less reliable, always relying on the other sex, which is strong, dependable and always professional.

Despite the sexist flaws in the original series, there are many feminists who are fans and who ignore or curse those flaws now. They are not prepared to do so with future scripts. We look forward to an improved <u>Star Trek</u>, one which we can relate to and not feel alienated by.

As an ardent feminist and a research librarian who has done extensive study of the program and the fan publications, I would be interested in your comments and happy to assist you in implementing my suggestions.

Sincerely yours,
Margaret M. Bailey
Chatham Township, NJ

In many ways, Gene Roddenberry agrees with the above. Does he think that STAR TREK was male chauvinistic by today's standards?

"Yes, by today's standards, indeed it was," he states. "We didn't use women as strongly as we might have. We did have women lieutenants, women attorneys. We often fell into the trap of making the captain's secretary-valet (the yeoman) a woman. I think if we did begin today we would start off more advanced than we were able to at that time.

"In my speeches, in my appearances around the country, I think that women's liberation is probably the question that comes up most often, and inquiries related to it are some of the most angry and critical questions I get. We're apt to get very angry, challenging questions, such as 'Isn't it true that you used women as sex symbols? You could see it in their costumes.' Yes, that is true. It came out of many things. It came out of the fact that I do see women as sex symbols. But the only defense I can offer is that in my younger years I was also seen by women as a sex symbol. I think that is part of the lovely fabric and the game of life. And I see nothing wrong with it. I think Bill Shatner with his shirt off in a show was very much a sex symbol to the females in the audience. I think there's nothing wrong with using women as sex symbols as well, as long as that's not the *only* way you're using women. If you're using them to the exclusion of their minds and attitudes and abilities and so on, that would be different . . . Also, we can't ignore the fact that I was playing to a 1964–66 audience with a large group that would enjoy seeing women in a setting not too different from what was the norm *then* and would be pulled close to the show by seeing those things.

"Would I change that? I think not a great deal, although we talked about having more women around and giving them better assignments, but would I change these sexual things? No. I think they're great fun."

What does he think of the miniskirts? Were they impractical?

"That may be so. Incidentally, we didn't take our miniskirts from the miniskirt craze. The miniskirt craze came in about a year after we had designed them. And I think there should be a little bow to Bill Theiss, our costume designer, who made those costumes very, very effective for women as well as for men.

"Also, you cannot produce a television show using

continuing male actors without having some pressure from them to be playing opposite lovely, sensual, sexual women. There is a continual pressure from actors: 'Hey, let me win the girl now.' And they get a charge out of playing a character who is so masculine, aggressive, and charming and so on that he wins the girl. It's an ego trip, but that's not a very bad thing. It's like sitting around in your daydreams and saying, 'Wow, wouldn't it be fun for me to win that man or that woman. The things I could do if I really put on the charm.' And for the actor it's the same kind of feeling.

"I was also playing to people who were unsympathetic toward the Women's Liberation Movement or who are made to feel uncomfortable by it, so I couldn't have women's liberation there at every moment in every scene. Remember, STAR TREK was in a mass medium playing to a mass audience, and I couldn't give more than a fair amount of time to any one viewpoint."

The STAR TREK philosophy—love, understanding, fair play for all in a future where races, religions, nationalities, men, women, and aliens are stirred together in the melting pot and emerge *people*—was a message that Gene tried to convey with great subtlety, and, I might add, with great success. Even young children were able to pick up on the nuances that made STAR TREK a different kind of show. As one child put it:

```
  I like Star Trek because Spock has
green blood, and because I like the
names.
```

In very simple terms, she stated what the STAR TREK philosophy is all about.

Chapter Three

The Collector

Please send me an autographed
picture of the U.S.S. _Enterprise_.
—Fifteen-year-old boy

To millions of enthusiastic fans, STAR TREK is more than just a television show: It's their full-time hobby. There are clubs to join. (STAR TREK Welcommittee's twenty-page directory lists 146 official clubs in the U.S., eight in Canada, six in England, one each in Mexico and Germany. Hundreds more exist unofficially the world over.) There are conventions to attend, lately as many as four a month. There are autographs to acquire. There are books, models, toys, games, kits, clothing, lunchboxes, records, pictures, and so on, all sold by companies licensed by Paramount Pictures, the company that controls the entire STAR TREK property.

Stephen E. Whitfield's book *The Making of STAR TREK* (Ballantine Books, 1968) and David Gerrold's *The World of STAR TREK* (Ballantine Books, 1973), both very popular with the fans, refer to a company called STAR TREK Enterprises. Now called Lincoln Enterprises, it was originally established as a fan service to try to answer questions, supply pictures of the stars, and the like. Today, however, Lincoln Enterprises' monthly mail volume is in the thousands, and the company is no longer able to answer individual requests for information (e.g., how did the cloaking device work, what is Spock's other name, where is the next convention). Currently a mail-order company, Lincoln Enterprises is licensed to sell pictures, bumper stickers, pencils, T-shirts, film clips, and the like. Some hobbyists think Lincoln sells *everything*, though, and the company gets some pretty strange requests. For example, one child wasted no time in trying to claim the U.S.S. *Enterprise* for her very own:

Dear Sirs:
 I would like to know if you could send me any parts of the <u>Enterprise</u>. Mostly I would want the bridge, Transporter Room, Engine Room, the Hangerdeck or the Conference Room.

Other fans are willing to settle for something a bit smaller, like the child who wrote:

 I would like to have a full size 8 × 10 portrait of the <u>Enterprise</u>.

Or the fan responsible for the epigraph to this chapter, asking for an "autographed" picture of the U.S.S. *Enterprise*. Perhaps the *Enterprise* could autograph an 8 × 10 portrait for him?
 Another *Enterprise* enthusiast wrote:

 Could I have a picture of the U.S.S. <u>Enterprise</u> firing its phasers at a Klingon battle cruiser and hitting it in color?

One fan wrote and asked about *other* fans, apparently worried that she might have fallen victim to some new disease:

 Do all <u>Star Trek</u> fans have this obsession about the series? It struck me as I was standing in line to buy the packaged blueprints for the U.S.S.

<u>Enterprise</u>,* "Am I nuts? What am I going to do with them?" Who cares—it's all part of the fantastic effect of that show.

> Sincerely,
> Sue Baugh
> Chicago, IL

Another frustrated collector wrote:

> Someday I would like to seek out and explore space. I bought the exploration set for my birthday and my communicator broke, the glue wouldn't hold up on my phaser, and I can't find my tricorder. So I beg you to send me one real communicator from the U.S.S. <u>Enterprise</u>!

One collector got a bit carried away:

> I wish your company could send me a communicator, a tricorder and a fake hand phaser. I have seen Leonard Nimoy at the New York Coliseum. But I never got his autograph. This doesn't mean I want his autograph. I have seen him on the "$10,000 Pyramid." He played, shall I say, most logically. So as I end my letter, I say please do not forget what I requested.

Huh?

Some letters read like lists to Santa Claus. For instance:

> Please send me Captain Kirk-Wm. Shatner's address, phone # & picture.
> "   "   " Mr. Spock-Leonard Nimoy's address, phone # & picture.

---

* Ballantine Books, 1975.

"   "   " Dr. McCoy-DeForest Kelley's
                address, phone # & picture.
"   "   " Scotty-James Doohan's
                address, phone # & picture.
"   "   " Chekov-Walter Koenig's
                address, phone # & picture.
"   "   " Nurse Chapel-Majel Barrett's
                address, phone # & picture.
"   "   " Lt. Uhura-Nichelle Nichols's
                address, phone # & picture.
Please give me a picture of the Engineering section. And all of their autographs too. Give me a list of all the
starships, and all of the enemy ships,
and all of the planets' names, and all
of the space stations' names, and all of
the stardate numbers, and all of the
starships' captains, and all of the
starship instruments and weapons, and
all of the enemy instruments and
weapons. I already have The Making of
Star Trek. Please hurry!

Many letter writers request phasers, tricorders, communicators, and medical kits—products Lincoln hopes to offer for sale eventually. Some people have very specific requests on the above:

If you could, send me a full-sized
hand phaser (in pistol mount) that was
used by the actors on Star Trek. How
much would it cost, postage and all?
Also could you send me a tape with the
sound effects of: 60 seconds of phaser
fire, 60 seconds tricorder, phaser on
overload, communicator beep, red alert
sound on Enterprise for 240 seconds;
whine of engines when under strain, 95
seconds; hiss of Dr. McCoy's hypo,
photon torpedoes, 100 seconds; trans-

porter hum, 30 seconds; door sliding
open, turbo lift, 100 seconds; various
sounds of control buttons when pressed
on bridge, 200 seconds. If so how much.
Please rush me your answer.

P.S. You may lengthen the time on
above tape to fill it on one side or
both sides.

Another phaser request came from an Ohio girl:

Do you know where I can get a phaser
to use on my stupid little sister when
she wants to watch Wonderful World of
Disney instead of Star Trek?

Danny Lee Kuchynka of Lawton, Oklahoma,
seemed to be having a similar problem:

I watch Star Trek all the time, but my
sister Tammy doesn't like it and I don't
know why. But I guess that is just the
way girls are.

William Shatner (and often his *shirt!*) is the subject of much mail:

Kirk's green shirt distinguished him
from the others on Star Trek.

o

When Kirk is in a fight and rips his
shirt, and you do not want it, I will
take it. Anything that you do not need I
will take. Anything!

o

If you could and will you please send

me anything from Star Trek. Like a ripped shirt that William Shatner wore on the show or a broken phaser or a Klingon shirt.
P.S. Please send me something good.

○

Please give me William Shatner's address* and James Doohan. Thank you.

Spock's ears get a lot of attention in the mail:

I was wondering, are you selling or giving away Spock ears? If you are doing the latter, would you please send me some. I want to scare my teacher. If you are doing the fore one, how much are they?

○

Please send me a pair of female Vulcan ears, at least for a graduation present. One of my life's ambitions is to wear them at commencement when I receive my diploma. The other is to meet L. Nimoy in person. (We can all dream, can't we?)
Yours sincerely,
Bobie Reyes
Houston, TX

Collectors will ask for almost anything:

I'd like to know if you could send me one of those gloppy things from "Operation Annihilate," or a Horta egg.

---

* The addresses of *all* the "regular" STAR TREK personnel are listed in the Appendix.

Finally, two rather unusual requests were sent to Helen Young of the Welcommittee, who shared them with us:

Dear Mrs. Young,

Although my friend Valerie and I live on different star bases, we are united by our love of Star Trek. You might say we are on either side of the Romulan Neutral Zone, thanks to the Klingons, masquerading as our parents. But, with subspace radio we manage. I hope you receive my message before our new code is broken. Please rush our order, because we are expecting a Klingon attack any minute.

> Live long and prosper.
> Jo Bellulovich &
> Valerie Saitas
> Brooklyn, NY

○

Dear Mrs. Young:

Enclosed is 50¢ of your Terran currency, and a self-addressed envelope. Please send me a Star Trek fan club directory. You see, on my native planet, there are no fan clubs, and Star Trek reruns ran out two of your Earth years ago. Therefore, since my love for Star Trek is exceeded only by my love for salt, I have been forced to your planet to seek out new clubs and new fanzines. I believe an appropriate term would be, "Thank you."

> Sincerely,
> The Great Salt Vampire

Chapter Four

The Stars and Their Characters

Could we be called "Scotties"?
    —Pair of James Doohan fans

Of all the inquiries received by Lincoln Enterprises and the STAR TREK Welcommittee, the overwhelming majority involve requests for information on the stars of the television show and the characters they portrayed. Of these, the center of attention, naturally, is William Shatner, who so aptly portrayed Captain Kirk. Here is a sampling of some questions and remarks about the good ship *Enterprise*'s sexy captain:

Dear Captain Kirk,

My son Jim has been a fan of yours and the crew of the Enterprise since he could sit up and watch TV. He collects space memorabilia, has read The Making of STAR TREK and the "Log" books and probably blasts off every night when he goes to sleep.

I cannot honestly say I'm a fan of yours, just a very tolerant mother. Our dinner time revolves around your program. It has to be before six or after seven if we want my son to sit at the table. We have given up fighting over it and just accept you as part of the family.

Please, Captain Kirk, send me your picture and autograph for Jim's birthday. Thank you and beam down into my kitchen anytime.

Sincerely
M. Sperling
Lincoln Park, NJ

Star Trek Day: opening of exhibit at Movieland Wax Museum, Buena Park, California (September 19, 1974). Clockwise from the upper right: William Shatner, Nichelle Nichols, Gene Roddenberry, Majel Barrett (Mrs. Gene Roddenberry), Leonard Nimoy, DeForest Kelley. Photo courtesy of Movieland Wax Museum and Norton Photography.

William Shatner prepares for a take in the third and final season of Star Trek.

○

Captain Kirk should not like every girl on the ship. It makes him out to be a pervert and he is not.

○

I would like to know why if Yeoman Rand and Captain Kirk really love each other, why don't they show it more than once?*

○

William Shatner is my favorite actor. I saw him on The Rookies. Believe me he's a great captain but he's a stinky cop.

○

I also like William Shatner as Capt. Kirk. If you meet up with him someday, please tell him I envy him and all the cute girls on Star Trek.

○

Even though Leonard Nimoy was good, you [Shatner] were the greatest. You fit the part like a shoe, not meaning that you are a shoe.

○

How old was William Shatner when he started to act in Star Trek? How old was he when he stopped acting in Star Trek?

---

* See p. 181 gentle reader.

Leonard Nimoy (left), George Takei, and Walter Koenig (right) at the Chicago Convention in 1975. Photo by Janet Smith.

Next in popularity is the *Enterprise*'s First Officer, Mr. Spock, played superbly by Leonard Nimoy. Some of the more "fascinating" questions about him:

Can Leonard Nimoy really move his eyebrow?

○

Is there any way that I could get the fanzine that has the nude picture of Spock in it?*

○

I like your show <u>Star Trek.</u> It is a good show. Mr. Spock is funny looking. But when he is not working he is not funny.

○

---

* I'm curious about that myself!

So far my room is done in "Star Trek Modern" (posters, etc.). I have 20 out of 23 books and I belong to a fan club. Even my clarinet has Spock ears!

DeForest Kelley, who played Dr. McCoy, recalls his most unusual fan letter:

"I received a letter that was very tightly sealed. Inside the envelope was a square of cardboard, and taped to it was a marijuana cigarette from a young lady who said that I had been turning her on, and now she wanted to return the favor!"

Another letter to De made reference to his "schnoodle"—his pet dog, half schnauzer, half poodle, mentioned in *The Making of STAR TREK*.

Dear Mr. Kelley,
I read that you have a schnoodle. We have one too. Her name is Princess. Reading that came as a bit of a sur-

DeForest Kelley outside the soundstage where TV's Star Trek *was filmed.*

prise, because I had thought Princess was unique. I've also got a hamster who I have named Montgomery James Bones Spock Roddenberry Scott. Scotty for short.

> Sincerely,
> Mari Blakely
> Richmond, VA

Scotty (James Doohan) is extremely popular with the fans. In a recent letter some New Jersey fans asked:

> I saw in a <u>Star Trek</u> book that Spock fans are called "Spockies." We both love Scotty. So could we be called "Scotties?"

Ensign Chekov (Walter Koenig) has great appeal to many young people, perhaps because they can

James Doohan (Scotty) at the Chicago Convention, 1975. Photo by Janet Smith.

identify with him as the youngest crew member on the bridge. Here are some of the interesting "Chekov" letters:

> On the cartoons, why don't they draw Chekov? Is he just too cute for them to draw?

To make best use of the special effects allowed by animation (especially in the creation of aliens), the part of Ensign Chekov was omitted and those of M'Ress and Arex, both aliens, were added. Walter Koenig did have an important behind-the-scenes role in the animated series—he wrote the script for "The Infinite Vulcan."

> My 13-year-old sister loves you. Many people saw you kiss a fan during the signing of the autographs. I told my sister and she blew up.

○

> Dear Paramount Pictures,
> Would you please send me a picture of Anton Checkoff?

○

> You ought to have part of that deck that Gene Roddenberry mentions in The Making of STAR TREK where they have the picnic tables with the real breeze and trees, the one like the big park. And the life support system could be damaged by a Klingon ship that sneaks a sudden attack and the regulars and some extra crew members could be sitting at three or four tables. The winds could start and the overhead sprinkling system that

waters the plants and trees could rain
and they could be trapped in there while
the Klingons would be attacking, and
Kirk could radio what to do to Chekov on
the bridge, cause Chekov is a Kirk in
training and he could save the day.
                              Sincerely,
                              Robert Ruiz
                              Arbuckle, CA

Walter himself says he has received over ten thousand letters. Of these, he recalled two that he especially liked:

"Most fans know I'm Jewish and I get a lot of religious tracts in the mail from fans who are trying to convert me. I remember a letter from a fourteen-year-old girl whose friend told her that Jews don't go to heaven. She was concerned and wanted to know what happens to us when we die. I told her we go to a small island off the coast of France where we eat mangoes and peanut brickle!

"I also received a letter from a concerned Mormon who said that since Bill [Shatner], Leonard [Nimoy], Harlan [Ellison], and David Gerrold and I were all Jewish, she wanted to convert us. I wrote and told her yes, but so were Dutch Schultz, Mickey Cohen, and Badeye Salutsky!"

Other characters also elicit some interesting comments:

Why is Sulu always wearing other crew
members' insignias on his shirt patch?

The only reason we could think of is that perhaps his shirt was still at the laundry and he didn't want to offer Bill Shatner any barechested competition! (Actually, Sulu always wore his own engineering insignia.)

Would you please send me a character

George Takei (Sulu) *in captain's chair on mock up of the Bridge of the* Enterprise *at the Chicago Convention in 1975. Photo by Janet Smith.*

Majel Barrett Roddenberry (Nurse Chapel) *addresses the audience at the New York Convention in February 1975. Photo by Janet Smith.*

THE STARS AND THEIR CHARACTERS

Nichelle Nichols (Uhura) *at the Chicago Convention in August 1975. Photo by Janet Smith.*

biography of Nurse Chapel (the way she talks, eats, etc.) and an autographed picture.

○

I just wish Uhura was played up a little more. All she does is open hailing frequencies and things like that.

○

Is there a chance of getting a photo of Mariette Hartley? She used to be on the <u>Star</u> <u>Trek</u> series and now I see she is doing the Tollhouse cookie commercials.

Mariette appeared as Zarabeth in the episode "All Our Yesterdays." Write to her at The Mariette Hartley Fan Network, c/o Rusty Hancock, 1649 Longfellow Ct., Rochester, MI 48063.

Even those villains you love to hate haven't been forgotten by the fans:

Dear Gene Roddenberry,
I am a <u>Star Trek</u> fan (or rather a freak). I think that the Klingon ship design is very modern in design and that does not mean that I want the Klingons to win. But they are very modern. And another thing is that you should put the Klingons in more episodes.
Sincerely yours,
Linky Klapper
New York, NY

Some general comments from fans included these:

If you could, I would like to have some pinups (free) from <u>Star Trek</u>.

○

Can you get me these autographs: William Shatner, DeForest Kelley, James Doohan, Gene Roddenberry, George Takei. Only get the ones you can get.

○

Let's put it this way. We're not in love with Captain Kirk, Mr. Spock, or Doctor McCoy. We love the Starship <u>Enterprise</u>.

So does Captain Kirk!

The Making of STAR TREK has become the bible of the STAR TREK cultists. Many letters refer to some of the unusual things first reported in that book, such as Bill Shatner's early "starving actor" days, when he was forced to live on, and developed a distinct aversion to, fruit salad, cringing at the very words themselves. Concerned fans wrote:

> By the way does William Shatner still get violent at the mention of fruit salad?

○

> Mention the words "fruit salad" and tell me how William Shatner reacts!

○

> Tell the captain I hate fruit salad too!

The book also revealed some startling information on the props—specifically, that there is more to Dr. McCoy's medical instruments than meets the eye:

> It's amazing what Dr. McCoy can do with salt shakers. You must dress them up a lot.

A reference to associate producer Bob Justman's unique way of getting Gene's attention, by standing atop GR's desk:

> Has Mr. Roddenberry ever had to have his desk refinished because of scuff marks on the top?

And a fan concerned over reported pranks which

"It's amazing what Dr. McCoy can do with salt shakers..."

centered around hiding Leonard Nimoy's studio bicycle:

> Do they still hide Leonard's bike? If they do, tell him I suggest strongly that he tie it up!

Finally, Gene Roddenberry, who receives close to one hundred letters a week himself, recalls his most memorable one:
"The one that affected me the most was from a university student, and it really affected me very, very strongly."

> Dear Mr. Roddenberry,
> It is my pleasure to tell you that if it were not for your program <u>Star Trek</u> being aired at the time it was, that I probably would not be in college at this moment.
> While I was in high school I was unsure of my future. I did not know if college was what I wanted or not. "You are not college material," they kept telling me! Then <u>Star Trek</u> came along and gave me courage to reach out and attempt something that everyone told me was impossible. I had <u>no</u> chemistry, physics, biology, trig. or any form of college preparation. Yet, encouraged by the character Mr. Spock and the way he brought himself up through the ranks, I was inspired to achieve what I have today.
> I now hold a B.S. in Secondary Education in Earth and Space Science. I am president of the Clarion Geographical Society, and president of the local chapter of Gamma Theta Upsilon, a worldwide organization in the field of geog-

raphy. Presently I am working on my master's degree in Science Education and specializing in Planetarium Education.

I most sincerely thank you for <u>Star Trek</u> and all it has done for me and my life.

                Sincerely,
                James Brown
                Graduate Assistant
                D. D. Peirce Planetarium
                Clarion State College
                Clarion, PA

Chapter Five

A Fan Is Born

I have been a fan since
I was able to walk.
—Nine-year-old boy
from Oklahoma

Flash! Another closet Star Trek fan comes out into the open!

So writes Patricia Brodin of Minneapolis. She and thousands of men, women, and children have suddenly discovered the joys of expressing their love for a television program that was canceled several years ago because, the network said, nobody was watching it! Today these "nobodies" include housewives, business executives, doctors, civil servants, toddlers, senior citizens, and, yes, even television executives. A recent article by Bernie Harrison in the *Washington Star* reported on a survey conducted by the Broadcast Information Bureau, which asked more than three thousand television executives and their families to name their personal all-time favorite shows. The responses listed 302 different titles. STAR TREK was ranked *third!**

What prompted these "closet Trekkies" to suddenly speak up and roar so loudly? Gene Roddenberry thinks the press may be adding impetus to STAR TREK's recent popularity.

"There have been front-page articles in the *Wall Street Journal*, the Los Angeles *Times*, *The New York Times*, and other papers. It's talked about now in news magazines. In 1966 or 1969 this would have been incredible. If anyone had told me it would hap-

---

* The top ten were: *Perry Mason, Your Show of Shows,* STAR TREK, *Playhouse 90, The Mary Tyler Moore Show, The Defenders, The Milton Berle Show, Omnibus, Monty Python's Flying Circus,* and *The $64,000 Question.*

pen, I would have considered him a far-out nut! Some of our fans think that the public has just awakened to the fact that STAR TREK is a gem—all things to all people. Well, perhaps that's part of it.

"Why did these people get interested in STAR TREK? At the beginning they weren't. It took awhile for all of this to build up. But over the years we saw a steady rise in the number of businessmen and politicians and professors and so on who began to write and began to be interested in STAR TREK. STAR TREK and science fiction became respectable."

According to Jeannette Abel, an Oakland, California, fan with a nineteen-year-old daughter, Trekkies are almost as abundant these days as tribbles (those furry little creatures in "The Trouble with Tribbles," which are born pregnant, multiplying faster than champion rabbits). Mrs. Able writes:

> I wasn't surprised to find two Trekkies in the variety store. My doctor's office "girl" is one. There is one in my peridontist's office and one in my regular dentist's office. Our veterinarian is one. And grocery store clerks.

April Pentland works for the Worcester (Massachusetts) County Institution for Savings and describes herself as "secretary-receptionist-cum-gopher." She sent us a lovely letter, using her office's stationery. She later noted:

> My boss was horrified to find me typing such a letter on company letterhead and doing it on company time, but he apparently admired my nerve, and is also enough of a fan to be able to quote entire episodes verbatim—at present he is attempting to requisition communicators for the office staff—and occasionally refers to me as Spock.

Joseph R. Morency is Zoning Administrator for Delhi Township, Hamilton County, Ohio. He sent a letter, on official Delhi Township letterhead, to the Welcommittee:

Dear Gentlebeing:

Okay already! I give up I can't stand it any more. I have watched Star Trek till my TV collapsed, I've read all eleven Blish adaptations, all four of the animated series, The Making of STAR TREK, The World of STAR TREK, The Trouble with Tribbles, and now (the final straw) STAR TREK Lives. I can't take any more. Please send me your directory and anything else you send us poor unfortunate Star Trek addicts. May The Great Bird of the Universe produce an episode just for you.

                      Sincerely,
                      Joseph R. Morency
                      Delhi Township, OH

Dennis R. Brightwell, M.D., an Assistant Professor of Psychiatry at the University of Kentucky, wrote us a letter back in 1972, when he was working in the Department of Psychiatry of the University of Iowa:

Dear Sir:

I would like to add my voice to the millions who have called for the revival of Star Trek. Its integrity, adherence to detail, and scientific realism made it unparalleled in television science fiction.

I try to watch local reruns, but the station's scheduling time at 4:00 P.M. makes it impossible for a professional person to be at home then.

I only hope that Star Trek will be revived, and in as close to the original proven form as possible. My compliments to you for being involved in this exciting project when first produced. I ask now that you will have the courage to begin again.

Yours very truly,
Dennis R. Brightwell, M.D.
Iowa City, IA

Gene Roddenberry recalled a time when professionals were not so forward-thinking:

"I think one of the best ways to illustrate the changes in attitudes that have happened is with something that happened to me. In STAR TREK's first year, after it had been on for maybe ten episodes, a former law professor of mine invited me to his club, the Harvard Club of Los Angeles, to be a guest and their luncheon speaker. It's their custom to have lunch and, they hope, hear something interesting and thought-provoking to carry away from the gathering. Well, I gave a talk to this group in 1966, and it was a disaster. My talk wasn't much different from talks I give now, but the attitude in those days was so different. These businessmen, bankers, insurance agents, and attorneys were looking at each other, saying, 'Who invited this nut?' 'This is not what we get together for, to hear insanity like this! What is he, on LSD?' I've never faced a less enthusiastic group. At that time, man hadn't been to the moon yet, and STAR TREK was considered a kid's show; science fiction was considered something for kooks. These men wanted to hear about reality.

"Now this whole thing has changed. Last year I was invited by my dentist to be a guest speaker at a Rotary Club luncheon, and it was totally different. I was facing almost exactly the same kind of audience I had faced nearly ten years earlier. But their interest in it was such that they made it a special Wives' Day.

There was enormous enthusiasm; a dozen people came to the podium with questions after the initial presentation. *I* had not changed, and what I was saying had not changed. But the whole attitude had changed 180 degrees, not only toward STAR TREK, but toward the future and science fiction."

Another career-oriented STAR TREK fan wrote this unusually expressive letter:

Dear Mr. Roddenberry,

I feel almost sure that by now you are quite tired of hearing about Star Trek and how great many of us think that it is. But I still feel an undeniable urge to add my words to the millions you have already received.

First let me reassure you that I am not one of the teeny-bopper fans (would that I was). I am a 29-year-old wife, mother, and barmaid. (Yes, barmaids do lead normal, no-booze programmed lives, too.) My husband is general manager in charge of advertising and sales promotion for a company based in Wixom, Mich. We have four children: Charles, age eight; Eric, who is seven; our only daughter, Whitney, age six, and our baby, Ian, who is four. We also boast two dogs, four cats (at the present time), a six-and-one-half-foot snake, and a three-and-one-half-foot iguana. Your typical American family, right?

We are even more typical in that we are avid fans of Star Trek. It has only been a few years since I began watching the show. Before that I was working and could only hear of it through others' viewing habits. It has been even more recent that I have discovered that there is a whole world of Star Trek which is very much alive and functioning. I now find that I have become an active part of that world, and a damn nice place it is too. But of course you already know that, since you created it.

It makes me believe that you must be a very special person. I refer especially to the "IDIC"* concept that you have created. Now I do not intend to sound melodramatic, but for me the IDIC has most certainly become a way of life. What it did to "get my head together" is more than my doctors could do in years. Mr. Roddenberry, they have given you and your IDIC credit for what I have accomplished. For bringing me back from a world where I could not cope because I was different from the woman next door or the guy down the street. You have taught me that being different is not to be wrong. You have also taught me that it is my duty to combine my differences with others to create for both of us. And so, Mr. Roddenberry, I say thank you, as you have never been thanked before.

> Live long and prosper,
> Mrs. Charles F. Kull, III
> Detroit, MI

Another businessperson, a management expert, writes:

Dear Mr. Roddenberry,
For reasons that I can't remember at the moment, I was out every single <u>Star Trek</u> evening during the initial run. I

---

* For the uninitiated, IDIC (Infinite Diversity in Infinite Combinations) is the Vulcan philosophy that the glory of the universe is in its incredible variety.

used to hear my kids talking about it, but who pays attention to kids? Because of the reruns, I think I have seen most of the episodes by now and if there are re-reruns, I'll be there.

I am a personnel management specialist with the U.S. Civil Service Commission—an "expert" (partly self-ordained, of course). This gives me a specialized point of view as I observe a lot of things, among them a particular <u>Star Trek</u> episode. I don't remember the name of the episode, but it centered around a malfunction of the transporter mechanism which caused two Captain Kirks to return to the Enterprise—one good, one evil.* As a student and observer of the management process, my reaction was that this episode could have been commissioned by the American Management Association as a training device. It portrayed better than anything I have ever seen the fundamental guts of command (or management) decision-making.

A couple of management professors whom I know have identified (and verified through observation of a number of successful naval officers) three attributes which seem to be commonly possessed by talented, genuine leaders:

1. A quality of sensitivity which is usually known as "feminine intuition."
2. A high level of anxiety.
3. Ambition, energy, drive.

"Sensitivity" permits awareness of problems which others are oblivious to. "Anxiety" equals caring or worrying

---

*The episode is "The Enemy Within," by Richard Matheson.

about the problem; others withdraw neurotically or—"screw it; I'll look into it next week." "Energy" and "drive" carry through to resolution. Captain Kirk sure fits this bill.

> Sincerely yours,
> George H. Smith
> Evanston, IL

This is not the first time management training has been suggested in connection with specific STAR TREK episodes. According to Gene, "One of the most interesting letters we ever received on that subject was from WNYC-TV, the municipal TV station of New York City. One of the station's executives read *The Making of STAR TREK*, noting the way we kept people going and how we raised morale. *The Making of STAR TREK* became the bible for him on how to manage the station. I understand they borrow many of our techniques."

One letter that impressed me quite deeply came from a mother with an almost unbelievable, borderline-miraculous story to relate:

> August 1, 1975
>
> I am 33 and the mother of seven. I have a small story to tell you about my oldest son, who is ten now.
>
> When he was small (about two years old), <u>Star Trek</u> came on around his bedtime. Every Friday night he would climb up in my lap and watch it till he went to sleep.
>
> As he grew older it was the first program he recognized and he would come running in yelling "Captain and Mr. Big Ears!" I wonder what Spock would have said to that?
>
> To make a long story short, on March 7, 1974, Alfred was hit by a motorcycle.

He was taken to University Hospital in Birmingham, Alabama. At 2:00 A.M. the doctor called us into one of those little conference rooms and told us he had suffered damage to the brain stem, a narrow part of the base of the brain which controls all motor functions, including breathing, and that he would be dead before morning.

What miracle God granted to let him live, I don't know, but as time passed and he held on, the danger of his dying began to lessen. However, all his limbs began to draw up until you couldn't pull them down. They were like steel. His eyes were open, but saw nothing. The doctor said if he survived, he would be a vegetable for the rest of his life. He was fed by I.V. and tube feedings. They moved him in June to a rehabilitation center for four weeks to try and get some response, but when that failed they gave up and moved him to a nursing home.

About that time we moved here to Knoxville and it was five long months before we were able to get him moved up here in January.

He was in a room that had a TV and they kept it on all the time to keep him company. He had been here about a week and I was there one evening when <u>Star Trek</u> came on. Being a fanatic, I turned the station so I could listen to it, while I watched him. One of my favorites, "The Trouble with Tribbles," was on that evening. As the story progressed, I noticed that Alfred's eyes looked different, and I bent over to get a better look at them. In doing so I blocked the TV and I nearly died when he moved his head and eyes. It began to dawn on me that he could see the TV. After five minutes I called the R.N. on duty. When she came in and saw his eyes she ran to call the doctor. It took him ten minutes to get there from his home and about ten seconds to confirm that Alfred was truly conscious for the first time since the accident.

When the show was over Alfred began to slide back into semi-consciousness. But every night when Star Trek came on he woke up. The doctor ordered all therapy arranged for the time it was on.

Within a week they stopped the tube feedings and put him on a puréed diet. He began to gain weight and to remain conscious for longer periods of time. He began to stir when the news came on before Star Trek and would remain awake for over an hour after it went off.

It is now seven months since this started. Alfred no longer slips into semi-consciousness. He is alert and awake. He can move his left arm by himself, and his legs. And the therapists are trying to stand him up.

But everything stops when Star Trek is on.

I felt I had to tell someone connected with the show what it had done for my son. Perhaps the hope and optimism mentioned so often in connection with the show is the reason he decided to try harder.

Sincerely,
Mrs. Robert (Pam) Littrell
Knoxville, TN

Many older STAR TREK fans are beginning to voice

their opinions. Recently our mail contained this intriguing letter:

Dear Wonderful People:
I am 50 years old and the holder of two college degrees. I teach literature and drama in college. For various reasons, like teaching night school, I never discovered _Star Trek_ until it went into syndicated reruns on our local WKBD-TV. It is really a new experience for me.

My background and teaching experience takes me into an almost professional interest in good story-telling craftsmanship. This interest in science fiction and in literature craftsmanship twice takes me to _Star Trek_. What a remarkable thing this series is (present tense intentional).

Thanks for these masterfully created dramas, even if they make a liar of me. I was always one who said to my classes that serious storying was dead and TV was the box they buried it in, and that (as Frank Lloyd Wright once said), TV was chewing gum for the eyes. Now when I say that I have to use an *.

Cordially,
Frank G. Nolte
Lincoln Park, MI

Other young-thinking fans have now come forward to voice their thanks. Mrs. Fern Lynch of Santa Rosa, California, recently wrote:

Dear Mr. Roddenberry,
I am thrilled, as are thousands of others, that you intend to do a _Star Trek_ movie.

---

*Except _Star Trek_

A FAN IS BORN 103

> I have been watching since 1967. I
> have seen each one fifteen or twenty
> times. What impressed me the most was
> watching the development of each charac-
> ter until it seemed like there really was
> a Captain Kirk, Spock, Scotty, Sulu,
> Chekov and Dr. McCoy.
> I am sixty-five, with twelve grand-
> children. I hope in this day when heroes
> are so badly needed and imagination can
> leave this world of ours for something
> better, that we will be seeing all of
> you once again.
>
> Sincerely,
> Mrs. Fern Lynch
> Santa Rosa, CA

Another fan, also finding that STAR TREK knows no generation gap, writes:

> I listened to Star Trek from the be-
> ginning and found it fascinating. Luck-
> ily I am a born optimist and Star Trek
> agrees with and enhances my idea of the
> future. I am 63, but am still looking
> forward, not back.
>
> Yours sincerely,
> Rosamond F. Leuty

One charming letter is from a wide-eyed fan, a grandmother of fifty-plus years, who paints a picture of her family of three generations of STAR TREK fans:

> Dear Mr. Roddenberry:
> Thank you, dear sir. I am over fifty,
> have children of all ages. One son was
> in the Air Force for four years,
> watches Star Trek faithfully. In fact
> this very day we are to miss an hour of
> The Time Machine because it is on the

same time as Star Trek. We have never seen the like, even my ten-year-old son. I wish you could see my house when he plays Star Trek! It's a real duplicate of the Enterprise. He moves everything out of the way, then before we talk to him we have to see what shirt he has on. He has three shirts almost identical, as good as I could sew them with the insignias you sent him. I even had to sew the braid on the cuffs. When he makes the Enterprise out of my house, he uses my pizza pans to make the transporter beams. I had to buy six just for that reason.

The past is over. The future is on its way. Outside of movies The Day the Earth Stood Still, The Time Machine, and The War of the Worlds, Star Trek stands out front in the S.F. class. The future—my little boy only ten, my grandchildren younger but not by much! Star Trek is part of the family! I look at each of my children—grown, some married, my ten-year-old son, for an hour even my grandchildren—on the floor in front of the TV, wide-eyed. I never hear a peep out of any of them for an hour! We live that hour in the Enterprise along with Capt. Kirk and Mr. Spock. We are amazed at Dr. McCoy in his futuramic Sick Bay! We love Scotty's Irish brogue! [sic]

It looks as if Leonard Nimoy could teach us the value of logic instead of letting our feelings run away with us. He plays his part so perfectly.

The future is on the way. The future is shows like Star Trek! Times have changed. Star Trek is the kind of show that can make these changing times bearable. Thank you for so many hours of pleasure with all my children and grandchildren.

                        Mrs. D. Haight,
                        Detroit, MI

A younger STAR TREK fan wrote to tell us of her family's involvement with the show:

Dear Star Trek,
  I am, in fact, Captain James T. Kirk (Deborah White). I, Debbie White, am fourteen, and a freshman in Kinmundy (Il.) Alma High School.
  I am the head of the weirdest bunch ever. One Friday last year my niece, three nephews, and I needed something to do, so we formed the Star Trek club. Me, James T. Kirk, because I'm usually the leader. My niece, Nelda, Mr. Spock, because she can lead when need be and she's very level-headed, she seldom loses her temper. She's 11 years old. Robert, a 10-year-old nephew, is Mr. Sulu because he claims he can drive everything from my mini-bike to the car. James, a 9-year-old nephew, is McCoy for the simple reason he wanted to be. David, a 7-year-old nephew, is Mr. Scott because he likes to take things apart to find out what makes them tick . . . Then my grandmother, she's 69, joined as Yeoman Janice Rand. My 50-year-old mother joined as Nurse Christine Chapel. My 29-year-old sister-in-law became Lt. Uhura. My 31-year-old brother is Chekov. My father, who's 53, also joined.
  Bye from all of us,

                        Faithful Fan,
                        Debbie White
                        Kinmundy, IL

If there are letters about the older generation "playing" STAR TREK, the younger set is not about to be outdone. Many write that they play STAR TREK games. To them, the *Enterprise* is real—so real, in fact, that one child was worried about the five-year mission. He wrote:

> I have an idea for the Enterprise's toilets.

And he did. He even sent *extremely detailed* (he omitted nothing!) drawings of how they should function. And another fan may have also thought the *Enterprise*'s mission was to seek out new restrooms, writing:

> Why did the Enterprise have no johns aboard? Gene made everything so perfect, but no johns.*

One young fan expressed his semipatriotic feelings about STAR TREK this way:

> I am a 15-year-old boy, a lover of mom's apple pie and Star Trek! Seriously though, Mr. Roddenberry, I realize that you are a very busy man and that you have no time to fool around.

What happens to STAR TREK's child fans when they grow up? Do they move on to other things? Apparently not, as seen in the following group of letters:

> Dear Helen [of the Welcommittee],
> When I left school to "make my way in this world" I reluctantly followed my parents' advice and threw away all the

---

* What Gene may have missed, Franz Joseph did not. His *STAR TREK Blueprints* can help you locate all the toilets on board. (Yes, there's even one on the bridge.)

Star Trek stories I'd written, and gave my Enterprise model to some younger friends. I sadly missed them, and was thrilled, upon unpacking my new husband's belongings over a year ago, to find neatly packaged—his model of the Enterprise. Since then our interest has slowly been growing to the point where we now want to get re-involved in our Star Trek. Bless you for your directory idea. Had either of us known of it years ago, we would have never let our interest lag for even a day.

      Love ya!
      Jackie (& Joe) Seppy

○

Dear Mr. Roddenberry,

I felt I just had to write this letter to tell you what enjoyment your extraordinary series, Star Trek, has brought to me, over the years.

I've been a science fiction afficionada all of my reading life, starting with "The Boy Who Discovered the Earth," and working my way up through Heinlein, Bradbury, Harlan Ellison—all the S-F books I could get my hands on.

I've been sincerely devoted to Star Trek since 1966, when I was in high school. I can remember urging my father to exceed the speed limit, on my return trip from a college interview in Connecticut, to make it home in time for the show. And he did.

Since that time, I've done a lot of growing. I've attended the Juilliard School, and have graduated from Adelphi University in New York. I am now a working professional dancer, a N.A.B.E.T. script supervisor, a photographer, and a film-maker (I did a dance film which toured the U.S. in "The Red Balloon Film Festival"). And my appreciation for <u>Star Trek</u> is ever-increasing.

I admire the beautiful manner in which the shows are lit, the direction, the rhythm of the editing, the music, as well as the writing and the actors' characterizations.

One day, I hope to be considered an artist in my chosen field. Your enduring work, <u>Star Trek,</u> attests that you are an artist in yours.

> With much joy,
> Nancy Paris

When young STAR TREK fans go off to college, they seldom forget their former fan experiences. Even the students at the Air Force Academy in Colorado hold STAR TREK in special esteem:

The Nineteenth Cadet Squadron recently approved a new squadron patch designed by C1c Brent Glines, which includes a starship as the central figure. The attachment is a photostatic copy of the proposed patch. We are presently awaiting permission from Mr. Gene Roddenberry and from our own Uniform Board before allowing the one hundred members of the Nineteenth Cadet Squadron to wear the patch.

> Sincerely,
> Stephen M. Herlt
> C2c, USAF

I passed the letter on to Gene, who answered as follows:

Dear Stephen,
 You not only have my permission to use our starship on your squadron patch, but also my very best wishes to the entire group and its officers. May it convey good luck in carrying you all to places in both inner and outer space "where no man has gone before."
 It is a particular pleasure for me to grant this permission, since I once flew for our country in what was then known as the Army Air Corps, graduating in Class 42G from Kelly Field, and serving

through the war in both combat and Stateside assignments. I still get a sentimental and warm feeling when I hear the music and words "Off We Go . . ." and I'm sure that background had much to do with the creation of Star Trek.

>Fraternally yours,
>Gene Roddenberry

The persistence of the STAR TREK memory—it doesn't seem to fade from minds of people growing up, going away to school, graduating, marrying, becoming parents, succeeding in business, or even, in the case of the following two letters, after total withdrawal:

Since March of last year I have been living in Monterrey, Mexico. Every few months I come to the States for cat food and Star Trek.

>John E. Trybus
>Monterrey, Nuevo Leon, Mexico

Here in Ferriday (Louisiana) I cannot receive Star Trek any longer. But as with any fan, memory keeps it alive.

>Thank you,
>Shelton Stewart

Chapter Six

Star Trek and Education

There are quite a few of us at the junior high who watch Star Trek. The rest are inferior.

—Eighth-grader from Iowa

I

When I was a youngster growing up in the fifties under the watchful eyes of my parents and the television, the only things mentioned about TV were the evils it caused in the world, and, my parents thought, to my own well-being: "If you watch too much television, you'll need glasses!" (I did and I do.) "You'll forget how to read books." (I didn't.) "You'll get lousy grades in school!" (I made straight A's.) Television was the scapegoat for nearly every problem that plagued our youth—it caused acne, cavities, obesity, unpopularity, and dandruff. It caused young minds to turn to tapioca, pregnant women to miscarry, and unmarried women to get pregnant. Its educational uses included learning to count up to Channel 13, becoming proficient at turning round buttons and knobs rapidly, seeing how grown men looked in ladies' dresses (remember Uncle Miltie?), and discovering for oneself Sir Isaac Newton's laws (only Superman can fly, dummy).

Students today have it much better. Here and there, between the commercials for curing acne, cavities, obesity, unpopularity, and dandruff, there is an occasional television program which not only entertains but can also be deemed "educational." Although not intentional on its part, STAR TREK seems to be both entertaining and educational. We have received letters from students of every age, from teachers of elementary school through college, from librarians, prison instructors, military advisors, et al., all commending STAR TREK for its value as an educational tool.

Gene Roddenberry believes one reason is the "pop

James Doohan (Scotty) signs an autograph for a young fan at the Houstoncon in June 1975. Photo by Janet Smith.

culture" aspect of STAR TREK, which is useful to a teacher in getting the class's interest. "As one high-school teacher wrote me," says Gene, "she was trying to make some points to the class on the alienation of people, one from another, and it occurred to her that if she would make herself up as Mr. Spock and put on some pointed ears, this might get their interest. The class stood up and applauded! She had their attention riveted on what she was trying to say.

"Part of it also is that STAR TREK talks about the

future, and the same thing has happened in schools of all levels that has happened to the general public. When I went to college, and I think more recently, too, even ten years ago, colleges really did not give courses on the future. They gave a great deal of attention to the past, but it was rare that courses were found on where we were going. STAR TREK concerns that, and when the space program came along and people began to look out in space and toward the future, it became a useful vehicle for professors who wanted to talk about those things. At the beginning of the STAR TREK phenomenon there was not very much in the way of textbooks being published on this area, so STAR TREK was very useful.

"There are a number of courses I've had letters about that deal with the STAR TREK philosophy, and it really flips me out that they would give a college course on STAR TREK philosophy! I really can't see it as a body of philosophy. It wasn't meant to be; it was meant to have philosophy in it, but not be a *system* of philosophy. I guess it came to be considered one because, as producer and compulsive rewriter, in every episode I dropped in items of my personal philosophy. This personalizing at least gave a unity to what was being said in the show."

The educational uses of STAR TREK have become so popular recently that the STAR TREK Welcommittee has set up a special department called STEP (STAR TREK Educational Programs). The program is headed up by a capable young woman from Virginia, Janice Scott Preston. In a letter to our office, Janice describes her work as follows:

STEP, a department of <u>Star Trek</u> Welcommittee, is trying to gather information on how <u>Star Trek</u> has been used, by teachers or schools, in any manner, for any reason, and <u>why</u>. As to what started me on this project: Helen Young and I were discussing the few, but interesting letters that S.T.W. had been receiving, with hints that Star Trek had been used in schools for a teaching tool. I remarked to Helen that it would be interesting to keep a record of these letters, and see if we could find more information about this. Helen then created the department, and appointed me department chairman, because of my interest. Subsequently Helen gave me Mary Manchester as a co-worker and co-investigator. I involved my sister, Diane McClaugherty, as my at-hand aide. Diane is the one who is helping me organize the department.

Mary Manchester is a teacher herself, who had success in using Star Trek in classes, which is why she contacted Welcommittee and offered to help in any way she could.

Diane has three sons, one of whom has dyslexia.* Naturally, he hated to read— but we encouraged him to read the Star Trek books, and from that, science fiction. We had ample personal experience with Star Trek as an educational motivation. I was interested to see what others had found.

There are times when someone says, "I thought I heard that _____ University, or Professor _____, at _____, has used Star Trek in some way." That is when we take over, writing general letters to the school, hoping that the person who opens the letter will have the information as to what department, or which person, should get the letter.

I am developing the opinion that our

---

* An impairment of the ability to read.

STEP department might become a service for teachers who want to correspond with other teachers who have used S.T. That is the type of request that I am now receiving.*

One of the very interesting letters received by Janice was from an elementary-school teacher trying to reach some children whose minds seemed closed to all attempts. This teacher wrote about one little boy:

I'll call him "Paul," for reference use. He was seven years old, repeating first grade, and so frustrated and unwilling to participate that his anger was almost palpable. Little notes in his file had forewarned me that he was supposedly rude, belligerent, and unwilling to learn or try. He spent the first two weeks trying to prove the last two true.

The class began a "space unit," and when I asked how space looked to an astronaut, there were more than thirty blank little faces. Suddenly I said, "What do you see on the main viewscreen of the Enterprise?" Instant understanding! We discussed Star Trek for a few minutes and they began to decorate their unit folders. Except for Paul, who scrunched his up in a little ball. There was no more manila paper so I replaced it with another kind.

When I returned to my desk after recess, this unsigned picture of Mr. Spock was on it; and it could only have come from one child. It was his first effort in two weeks, and it was a very accurate portrait for a primary child. If he could do this . . .

---

* See Appendix for information on contacting Janice.

After a few days he began to copy boardwork, and he did so with great accuracy. That year he mastered the alphabet, began to read, and eventually became one of our finest math students. It was difficult for him to concentrate, and symbols were hard for him to remember, but he kept trying.

Soon he would beg to stay in at recess and lunch, then spend the whole time retelling the previous evening's *Star Trek* episode. In the beginning, every comment was about Spock or from Spock's point of view. It was obvious that Paul's deep response to the Spock character was a result of his feeling alone and different. But, because he felt this identification so strongly it was possible to use it to guide his social development. Something like teaching Ethics and Human Relations 101 with *Star Trek* as a text. Some kind and generous soul at Paramount read my query letter and sent me a small but well-filled box of stills and other goodies with which I could tempt/encourage/reward Paul's progress.

We role-played. We had little "group sessions" at lunch with Paul's peers as guests. He taped endless *Star Trek* stories for me and later shared them with the class. After only a few weeks he began to be able to deal with some of his own problems without putting them in an artificial construct. He began to deal with reality instead of hiding from it. Slowly, he began to learn some self-control and to feel some pride in his own accomplishments despite severe self-doubt.

All this did not solve all his problems, but perhaps it made life more bearable for him. At least he no longer played hookey.

What happened to him? That is a difficult thing to describe because it is a real tragedy. We have a good school, dedicated teachers, and a lot of support personnel. Most of all, though, we <u>care</u> what happens to our students. Somehow, Paul got lost that next year; and, even more sadly, no one seemed able to understand his need for psychological support until a year later, when he was placed in a special school.

It has been several years since I've seen him, but I'll never forget him. Even in that last year, when he wanted to talk he would hand me a drawing. It was always the same: Spock, alone on the bridge.

Gene Roddenberry finds particular pleasure in the uses of STAR TREK in helping unusual children, "whatever their reason for being unusual," says Gene. "For example, STAR TREK has been very useful to teachers in dealing with retarded children. It's the fairy-tale relationship, and the teachers see it as a way of talking about love, tolerance, and the like, and it's worked very well. The strange thing about it—and the delightful thing—is that it runs the full range. It's even helping to educate and change ideas and attitudes among mentally retarded children, and is used with exceptionally bright children.

"In this general area is another source of pleasure and some pride. It concerns a special division of STAR TREK fans. These are the fans whom life has treated unkindly in some way. It includes girls who feel they are really not pretty, those whom nature has made very heavy or lame, or those who have trouble

"When he wanted to talk he would hand me a drawing. It was always the same: Spock alone on the bridge."

with stuttering—people with emotional and physical difficulties. I'm terribly fond of this group of fans, because it's become apparent from their letters and from meeting them that STAR TREK represents to them a hope and a belief that some day we'll be wise enough not to judge them by their exteriors, that we will be able to see the beauty that is inside them. And these people have *great* beauty inside them. I'm anxious for a time when everyone will realize that. They watch Spock and say, 'Yeah, these people could see me and they would love me for myself rather than judge this body that's imprisoning me.' It's a good feeling to know that you're giving some joy that way."

A dedicated teacher working with exceptional children wrote us of her experiences in using STAR TREK:

Dear Mr. Roddenberry,

I am currently teaching a non-graded physically handicapped class outside of Philadelphia.

One of my students, David Singer, has been creating Star Trek stories since December of last year [1974]. David is a bright eleven-year-old boy who has been disabled with cerebral palsy since birth. He is confined to a wheelchair, but is able to do many things for himself. His main interests since I have known him have been reading and writing science fiction stories. Needless to say, these stories have provided a great impetus to improving his writing and typing ability, and have been used as the central point for reading and English lessons.

It's so much fun to watch this creative boy so absorbed in his stories. We discuss your show, talk about the stories, and he often reads them to the class. He gets so excited when he has a new idea for a story, and many afternoons he has asked to stay overnight to finish one!

David has asked me to mail his stories to you. He said, "Sorry about all the typing mistakes." I have assured him that you will certainly enjoy his ideas and typing is a minor part.

So you see, sir, your creativity through Star Trek is sparking more creativity. Thanks! Teaching and learning are so _much_ more fun when Captain Kirk, Spock and Sulu are involved.

>Sincerely,
>Kate Devlin
>Fairless Hills, PA

Here is what young David wrote:

Dear Mr. Roddenberry,
  I hope you like my stories.

>Sincerely,
>David Singer

This is a story about the _Enterprise_:

The Fire Ball Monsters

While flying in space the _Enterprise_ sighted a Klingon ship but the Klingons had a fire ball monster. They put up their shields. The fire ball monster threw a fire ball. They lost their number four shield. They shot their phasers. The Klingon's ship was gone. The _Enterprise_ won.

The End

David sent several stories, each showing growth and improved usage of writing skills. Space prohibits reprinting all of them here, but Gene's reply to David is worth noting:

>June 6, 1975

Dear David:
  Thank you for your _Star Trek_ stories, which I read and very much enjoyed. When I was a boy your age, I had a condition which made it very difficult for me to breathe and was unable to spend time out on the playground with others, so I spent much of my time reading and

writing stories as you are doing now.
I suppose I wanted to be a football hero
or something like that but, as it
turned out, I ended up having even more
fun from books and writing, and all the
wonderful friends I met through those
things.
   Keep up the writing and imagining!
                        Sincerely yours,
                        Gene Roddenberry

A letter from the director of the Lowell School in Flushing, New York, along with a report from a teacher of a gifted young boy, and Gene's subsequent answer, add to this new and exciting use of STAR TREK:

                        April 18, 1975
Dear Mr. Roddenberry:
   The enclosed is about an exceptionally
gifted 15-year-old who is a classic de-
velopmental dyslexic, à la Thomas
Edison, Niels Bohr, et al.
   In September he read "Jud Had a Big
Cat." With daily help with special
techniques, he now reads the enclosed
E.P.A. [Environmental Protection Agency]
material. To quote his special teacher,
"The person he most admires is Gene
Roddenberry. Roger can name the stories
this man has written, knows where he
was born, etc. Roger tells us if this
man told him that reading was an essential thing, he would try his hardest
to persevere."
   An autographed book (and please bill
us), a note from Mr. Roddenberry to
Roger? These would give this boy a
tremendous lift, and he is a boy who
will do something very interesting some
day . . . But Gene Roddenberry is the man

who matters. I hope we will hear from
you soon.
>   Cordially,
>   Harriet L. Blau
>   Director, The Lowell School
>   Flushing, NY

The material with Director Blau's letter included Roger Graf's reading material in September: "A pig had fun in mud," "Can a fat pig run in Mud?" and so on. By March he was reading from an EPA pamphlet: "Photochemical smog is a mixture of gases and particles oxidized by the sun from products of gasoline and other burning fuels." His teacher, Dorrie Silverstone, included his April word list:

> The following is the cumulative list that is comprised of self-chosen high level interest words. Roger has gotten 90-100% on all of his tests: ballistic, missile, cosmos, destruct, computer, energy, matter, destiny, operation, radiation, creation, gravitation, crystal, dormant, crypt, abnormal, reaction . . . [plus fifty other words, all basically science- and <u>Star Trek</u>-oriented.]
>
> Science fiction and science are Roger's main interests. He composes his own science fiction stories. At the beginning of the year he was extremely self-conscious, and would not attempt to write his stories. He used the tape recorder instead. He now writes long stories, using the phonetic method.

Gene answered as follows:

Dear Roger:
 I have been told of your exceptional

progress in reading during the last year and that you are especially interested in reading and writing science fiction. It was also suggested you might want to know how I feel about books.

First and most important, I consider reading the greatest bargain in the world. A shelf of books is a shelf of many lives and ideas and imaginations which the reader can enjoy whenever he wishes and as often as he wishes. Instead of experiencing just one life, the book-lover can experience hundreds or even thousands of lives. He can live any kind of adventure in the world. Books are his time machine into the past and also into the future. Books are his "transporter" by which he can beam instantly to any part of the universe and explore what he finds there. Books are an instrument by which he can become any person for a while—a man, a woman, a child, a general, a farmer, a detective, a king, a doctor, anyone. Great books are especially valuable because a great book often contains within its covers the wisdom of a man or woman's whole lifetime. But the true lover of books enjoys all kinds of books, even some nonsense now and then, because enjoying nonsense from others can teach us to also laugh at ourselves. A person who does not learn to laugh at his own problems and weaknesses and foolishness can never be a truly educated or a truly happy person. Also, probably the same thing could be said of a person who does not enjoy learning and growing all his life.

The reason I have written you such a

long letter is that we not only share a
love of science and science fiction, but
we share something else. When I was a
child, I was disabled by illness. Although my problem was different from
yours, it did keep me from enjoying many
things enjoyed by other young people.
In a way, this turned out to be fortunate for me, since it turned me toward
books. In those days, I used to think
that it would have been better to have
no physical problem and to have become
a great football star or something like
that. But now I realize that my love of
books gave me much more happiness than
anything else could have done.

Please do try your hardest to persevere at reading. You will never regret
doing that.

                Very sincerely yours,
                Gene Roddenberry

This letter from an inquiring teacher was received by Helen Young of the Welcommittee:

Dear Ms. Young:

I am interested in obtaining information about <u>Star Trek</u> and its fans.

I am also a teacher for handicapped children who are confined to the home and who are <u>Star Trek</u> fans.

I would appreciate it if you could send me whatever information is available.

                Thank you,
                John Sole

Helen forwarded the letter to Janice Scott Preston, who says, "I asked Mr. Sole for more information. He gave my request to one of his students." Here is what the student wrote:

*Nurse Chapel and Dr. McCoy search for a cure.
Photo by Janet Smith.*

Dear Mrs. Scott:
 Mr. Sole, as part of my homework assignment, asked me to watch Star Trek on Channel 11.
 Star Trek has been useful to me in that I have developed an interest in science fiction and from that an interest in science.
 Some aspects of the Star Trek series included the use of lasers, space medicine, astronomy, and the belief that there is intelligent life throughout the universe in many forms. Star Trek not only taught basic facts in science, but also that color, shape, size are not important in judging a person or another form (such as may exist in UFO's) on the basis of understanding, tolerance, com-

passion and respect. Also because of the
interest I developed in watching *Star
Trek*, I have read some of the books that
have been published (*Log One* through
Twelve). I have also read articles in
the *Enquirer* in which the Navy was
interested in the command center of the
starship *Enterprise*. I have read other
articles that show that medical technology is not too far away from some of
the medical instruments that Dr. McCoy
used in the starship *Enterprise*. An
example would be the table that measures
heartbeat, blood pressure and body
temperature.

Therefore, due to watching *Star Trek* I
have developed a keen interest in
science fiction, or science, and perhaps
one day I hope to play a part in the
space program.

Mr. Sole asked me to write to you
because he thought it would be more
valuable coming from a student of his
rather than coming from his own subjec-
tive point of view.

Yours truly,
Diane M. Cascello
Staten Island, NY

Intrigued by the wisdom and maturity shown by this student, I wrote to her personally, asking for more information about her. Here is her reply:

Dear Ms. Sackett:

In reply to your letter of October 15,
1975, I am 13 years old and I attend
Egbert Junior High School on Staten
Island. I am in the 8th grade.

At the present time I am on home in-
struction due to scoliosis. I have been

home since the spring of 1975 and I
probably will not return to school until
the winter of 1976.

In New York City the Bureau for the
Education of the Physically Handicapped
provides for home tutors for children
who are unable to attend school.

Mr. Sole is my primary teacher while
Mr. Garrison and Mr. Vicoli are special
subject teachers who teach math &
Italian.

I am interested in science—especially
astronomy and related areas. I intend to
join the Civil Air Patrol when I recover
from my disability.

I hope one day to be a scientist in
some field that would combine science
with health, such as aeromedical
research.

Sincerely yours,
Diane Cascello

II

1.

A youngster who found himself involved with teaching, though only briefly, had the following experience:

A little over a year ago when I was
helping teach a one-day course on UFO's,
we got into a bit on <u>Star Trek</u> and one
guy said he thought <u>Star Trek</u> was nearly
as good as <u>Lost</u> <u>in</u> <u>Space</u>. That's enough
to round Spock's ears!

A fan for life,
Michael A. Shepherd
Drakesville, IA

2.

Robert C. Gartner of Ocean Township, New Jersey, taught a course in STAR TREK during the 1975–76 school year. He was kind enough to share his outlined course of study with us:

Seminar in Star Trek

Time Allotment: 1 Quarter
Ability Level: 3 (Grades 10-11-12)

I. Basic Texts
   A. The Making of Star Trek
   B. The World of Star Trek
   C. The Trouble with Tribbles
   D. Star Trek Adaptations 1-10

II. Aims and Objectives
   A. Aims
      1. To become familiar with an important development in the genre of science fiction.
      2. To study human values as they are presented through science fiction, and more specifically through Star Trek.
      3. To evaluate 20th-century man as he is viewed from the vantage point of a future universe.
      4. To evaluate current social issues from the objective vantage point of a future universe.
   B. Behavioral Objectives
      1. Given a selection of literature, the student will be able to examine the social

issues presented and evaluate them as they apply to 20th-century man and his society.
2. Given a selection of literature, the student will be able to examine the characters and compare mankind of the future to mankind today.
3. Given a selection of literature, the student will be able to examine and compare the human values and morals of the future universe and our present universe.
4. Given a writing assignment, the student will be able to analyze and compare man's progress, society's advancement and the overall differences and similarities between Roddenberry's universe and our modern universe.

III. <u>Course Content</u>
 A. <u>Literature</u>
  1. Given certain pages from the resource books, the students should be able to learn as much as possible about Roddenberry's characters, ship and universe. This will serve as a solid foundation for comparison of the two universes.
  2. Given certain episodes from <u>Star Trek</u> adaptations, the students will examine the plausibility of the situations presented. Special emphasis should be placed on

the treatment of human
values, continuing social
concerns, etc.
B. Schedule
1. Week 1—Seminar in Star Trek
will begin with an explanation of the material to be
covered, the requirements of
the course and the grading
system to be used. The first
week will be spent intro-
ducing the universe of Star
Trek to the students. The
following books will help in
this area:

The Making of STAR TREK—pages 163-258
—Introduction of the Enterprise, its
crew, and its antagonists
or
The World of STAR TREK (Part I)

2. Weeks 2-7—Series adaptations
will be discussed in class
(one per day). Discussion of
these stories will center
around a detailed comparison
of the antagonists and the
protagonists and their comparison to modern man. Social
issues, moral values, etc.
will be discussed. The final
objective is to have the students objectively view the
future universe and make
objective analyses of our
modern society and modern
man. Suggested episodes are
as follows:

"Charlie's Law"

"Balance of Terror"
"Arena"
"A Taste of Armageddon"
"Errand of Mercy"
"City on the Edge of Forever"
"The Trouble with Tribbles"
"Mirror, Mirror"
"The Menagerie"
   (based on the first pilot)
"Let That Be Your Last Battlefield"
"Requiem for Methuselah"
"The Way to Eden"
"The Savage Curtain"
"The Apple"
"Who Mourns for Adonais?"
"The Paradise Syndrome"
"Where No Man Has Gone Before"
   (second pilot)
"The Ultimate Computer"
"Obsession"
"The Empath"
"The Omega Glory"

3. <u>Weeks 8-9</u>—Students will spend the last two weeks doing independent work. Choices are as follows:

<u>The Making of Star Trek</u>
<u>The World of Star Trek</u>
<u>The Trouble with Tribbles</u>

Students will choose one aspect from the book of their choice (ex.: characterization, structure of the <u>Enterprise</u>, antagonist vs. protagonist, etc.) and write a paper on this subject. The paper should be a summary of the course and should include

  items of discussion as well
  as the above reading assignment.
 4. Students will be encouraged
  to watch <u>Star Trek</u> and any
  science fiction which may
  relate to the course.

IV. <u>Methods of Teaching</u>
 A. Class Discussion
 B. Lecture
 C. Audio-visual Materials
 D. Guest Speakers when
  feasible

V. <u>Methods of Evaluation</u>
 A. Tests and Quizzes
 B. Compositions
 C. Contribution to Class
  Discussions

3.

Robert H. Gibbons of Springfield, Missouri, has taught a "minicourse" on the college level. The course was called "Physics 155—*Star Trek*." Bob explained: "The class was very small, made up of physics majors in a special problems course. They were all STAR TREK fans and of course this was during the run of the series. The course hours were spent watching the show and discussing the scientific aspects. I had a slide lecture at this time . . . This is the test I gave to my class. It isn't as hard as the trivia tests at the Cons, but more physics is required."

<u>Final Examination—Physics 155—
    Star Trek</u>

I. Discuss the theory and applications of:

Gene Roddenberry signs autographs for young fans after a college speaking appearance.

1. Sensors
2. Phaser banks
3. Deflectors
4. Tractor beam
5. Tricorder
6. Communicator
7. Library computer
8. Impulse engines
9. Transporter
10. Photon torpedo

  II. List five sister-ships of the <u>Enterprise</u>.
 III. List the officers and crew of the starship <u>Enterprise</u>.
  IV. Define warp factor.
   V. What is the maximum safe speed of the <u>Enterprise</u>?
  VI. What is the Federation? Who are the enemies of the Federation?
 VII. Describe the physical characteristics of the <u>Enterprise</u>, including size, size of crew, ration of males to females.

VIII. List five characteristics of a Vulcan.
 IX. Define star date.
  X. What is the mission of the <u>Enterprise</u>? How long is the assignment?

4.

Thomas Limero is a science teacher in Puerto Rico. He wrote:

> I am presently employed at the Caribbean School in Ponce, Puerto Rico, as chairman of the science department. I have been teaching high school for five years.
>
> During my years of teaching I have often speculated on the use of science fiction as a tool for the classroom. Last year I implemented a two week minicourse on future studies which relied heavily on science fiction films . . . I further visualize the employment of science fiction as a multidisciplinary teaching device reaching science, social studies, mathematics and English curricula. The <u>Star Trek</u> series presents a good example of speculative fiction which easily lends itself to teaching units in a multitude of areas.
>
> Collating these two facts—the rise in the use of science fiction and of visual media in the classroom—I would like to suggest for your consideration the possibility of utilizing specific episodes of the <u>Star Trek</u> series as a teaching device. This would be an interdisciplinary course involving at least high school science and social studies.

The advantages to such a program are evident:

1. An opportunity for the student to visually encounter some of the problems and delights of the future—changes that he may help create.

2. To expand the student's imagination and allow him to see how scientific principles of today may be put to use in the future.

3. Importantly, since the goal of schools is to prepare the student for <u>his future</u>, we would be studying science of the future and projecting it back to the present to gain insight to the possible implications of the science and social decisions of today.

4. It gives the student a sense of the close interrelationship between social and technological developments.

5. While careful scientific investigation is invaluable, imagination and creativeness are indispensable to a great scientist, and yet, these are the very things we often kill in high school science curricula. Hopefully this program would help keep these avenues open in the young people's mind.

The number of topics available boggle the mind; however, a few examples are:

1. The <u>Enterprise</u> engines lead to discussions of matter and anti-matter, $E=mc^2$, faster-than-light travel and time-space warps, to name a few.

2. The transporter would stimulate discussions on electron energy levels, and electrical activity in the human body.

3. The episode "Miri" leads to discussion of miracle drugs and immortality

with all its implications for society.

4. The episode "A Private Little War" has many insights into the role of the United States and Russia in the Middle East and Vietnam.

I am enthusiastic about creating a curriculum for such a venture and I would be willing to write the project during the spring and use my classes in the fall as a pilot program. Although I do not work with underachievers, this type of approach may also prove extremely successful in this area.

Thank you for your time and your consideration.

> Sincerely,
> Thomas Limero
> Chairman, Science Department
> Caribbean School
> Ponce, PR

Mr. Limero had requested STAR TREK films for use in his classroom, as have many teachers. Unfortunately, Paramount has had to maintain a strict policy on this, and films are not generally loaned, due to royalty requirements of the writers', directors' and screen actors' guilds. In a subsequent letter–progress report, Mr. Limero wrote:

Sept. 24, 1975

Dear Ms. Sackett:

As you may know my original idea has been stymied due to the fact that <u>Star Trek</u> films are unavailable for classroom use at a reasonable cost.

However, I have used various stories in biology and chemistry classes to illustrate topics such as evolution, like properties of chemical families ("The Devil in the Dark"), immortality and electron energy levels (working principles of <u>Enterprise</u> transporter).

In the spring I will offer a "Future Studies through Science Fiction Reading" course which will include several stories from <u>Star Trek</u> episodes.

You may find of interest one student's idea of utilizing a transporter such as that mentioned in <u>Star Trek</u> as a means of achieving immortality. The computer would store an individual's atomic energy levels and placement at age twenty. Every five years the person would use the transporter with the materialization programmed to the atomic energy levels and placement at age twenty, with the exception of the brain areas related to the accumulation of new knowledge. At this point the implications diverge in many directions. This type of reasoning indicates the student's ability to think logically and creatively when motivated.

       Sincerely,
       Thomas Limero

5.

Often when STAR TREK courses are lacking in the school curriculum, *parents* rather than teachers become strong proponents of such programs. One interested parent is Dolores Weinzimmer, a mother of four who wrote:

       January 22, 1972

Dear Mr. Roddenberry,

Basically, I'm hoping to see <u>Star Trek</u> used in the social studies curriculum, but I also think it could be stimulating in science and math classes as well. Social studies is especially in need of a new approach, and since the idea of looking backward is unpalatable to the administration, I have taken it upon myself to find a new idea which will please the powers that be and provide a stimulating learning experience for the kids. I have been in touch with a school in Chicago which has been using _Star Trek_, and they have had great success—sometimes the students there are so enthusiastic that the teacher finds it necessary to depart from the prepared text and opens the classroom for discussion.

Although you probably designed _Star Trek_ as a commercial venture, it has provided my own four children with more than entertainment. We have spent many evenings as a family discussing scientific theories as put forth in an episode. On many occasions our living room floor has been wall-to-wall encyclopedias after the television set was turned off. My twelve-year-old daughter is currently involved in presenting a report on matter and anti-matter; her interest is a direct result of "Lazarus." My ten-year-old son, who spends his allowance and earned money on models, has driven hobby shops and toy stores nuts trying to find a model of the _Enterprise_. When I recently came into possession of a much-used copy of _The Making of STAR TREK_, he studied the plans shown therein, hoping he might start from scratch, but finally had to admit it was beyond him. My eight-year-old son (also known in this house as

Captain Kirk) still carries his "communicator" (actually a deactivated cigarette lighter) in his pocket. His interest goes deeper than emulating the good captain, though—part of his birthday money went toward the purchase of a Little Golden Book on stars, and I recently received a call from his teacher, who thought I ought to know my son had asked why his third-grade science class couldn't study the solar system.

The seventh-grade school magazine, Read, makes reference to Star Trek from time to time when presenting information relating to space. Clearly, Star Trek is alive and well and living in many places.

Any ideas and suggestions you might have would be most welcome. If you don't have any, my sincere thanks anyway for a wonderful program which has done so much for so many. You have provided for my children (and countless others) an experience which has expanded their horizons, opened their minds to the wonders of the future, and stimulated their desire to learn. Thanks so much.

Very sincerely,
Dolores Weinzimmer
Glencoe, IL

I wrote to Mrs. Weinzimmer to see what had transpired in the more than three years since she had written that letter. Here is part of her answer:

October 12, 1975

What a flood of memories you stirred up. My youngest son is wading through the same tired curriculum his brothers and sisters endured. He "graduated" from

his make-believe communicator to a real
walkie-talkie, and then saved enough
money to buy a citizen-band set. His
C.B. "handle" is, very naturally, "Enterprise." His bigger brother did eventually find a model of our favorite
starship, and went on to more complicated projects—climaxed last spring
when he built a canoe—in the middle of
our living room (where else?)

All four of our children have developed a respectable knowledge of who's
who and what's where in the heavens;
they still watch <u>Star</u> <u>Trek</u> reruns on
Sunday mornings, even though there are
some episodes they have practically
memorized; they are acutely aware of
scientific discoveries, and agree with
my conviction that much of yesterday's
science fiction will be tomorrow's
science. You can tell Mr. Roddenberry
that our appreciation for his creative
genius and the effect it had on our
children grows deeper as we watch them
grow and learn and wonder and seek
answers. Our family "rap sessions" continue to bring the encyclopediae off of
the shelf. (In a house with four teenagers, that's not bad for communications.) This is a direct result of Mr.
Roddenberry's imaginative talent, and we
love him for it.

                                Sincerely,
                                Dolores Weinzimmer

6.

On the college level, there are several courses in
STAR TREK being given. Edward Jay Whetmore is an

Instructor in Communications at Lewis and Clark College in Portland, Oregon. Here is the course he gives to his freshman students:

Freshman Seminar

"The Making of STAR TREK"

Required Texts:
1. David Gerrold, The World of STAR TREK.
2. David Gerrold, The Trouble with Tribbles.
3. Nicholas Johnson, How to Talk Back to Your Television Set.
4. Marshall McLuhan, The Medium is the Message.
5. Edward Whetmore, Color TV: Thru the Looking Glass.

Gene Roddenberry at a typical college lecture. Often the crowds number in the thousands.

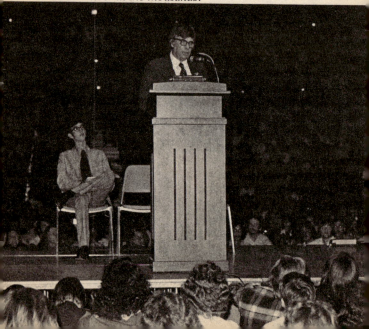

6. Stephen E. Whitfield, **The Making of STAR TREK.**

Course Objectives:
The average American will spend the equivalent of over 3,000 days, or nine full years, of his life in front of the television set. "The Making of STAR TREK" is a series of inquiries into the sociological effects of such consumption.

Star Trek is a logical point of departure for a number of reasons. Its unique characteristics will be compared with current commercial and non-commercial fare.

The seminar is designed for the consumer; that is, the primary academic goal is to obtain a critical perspective on the medium. Other considerations will include comparative efficiency studies with other media and an investigation of network rating structures and other variables which determine program content.

Description of Course:
The Concept: this will be an about-face in video learning. For, unlike television courses which move from the general to the specific, "The Making of STAR TREK" will move from the specific to the general.

Direct focus on one show will have advantages. From the first day of class students will be working with a known quantity. Their studies in the areas of story techniques and all phases of programming as well as various liaison problems (i.e., networks, production schedules, studio rental, packaging problems) will come from direct example of actual problems encountered in "The Making of STAR TREK."

Star Trek is an ideal vehicle for several reasons:

1. No one program in recent years has developed a more intense interest on the part of its viewing public. The "viewer demonstrations" that kept Star Trek on the air for a third season were unprecedented in network television history.

2. Seldom has a network show displayed so transparently the plot and ploy techniques (emotions vs. logic, duty vs. sensuality,, etc.) that are standard network fare.

3. Seldom do we have a text available which covers so completely the intimate details of a network production.

Input:
  Text: A. The Making of Star Trek, Stephen E. Whitfield
  B. How to Talk Back to Your TV Set, Nicholas Johnson
  C. Teleplay, Coles Trappner
  D. Handouts (research studies on effects of TV)

Output:
1. Weekly analysis papers of all aspects of episodes seen in class.
2. Written and oral reports on individual research.
3. The student will, by the end of term, be able to pass the following final exam:
   a. Describe in detail the transformation of a story idea to a net-

work program airing. Be specific
in the following areas:
1. teleplay techniques
2. story revision
3. production problems as they
affect the script
4. selling the network
5. network censorship
b. Through use of example, define
five leading plot techniques.
c. Choose one network program. Detail inherent internal plot-conflicts as we have discussed.
d. Choose one of the following hypotheses and support or refute
it based on the empirical studies we have read and discussed:
  i. TV violence begets "real
     life" violence.
 ii. TV's premissive sexual attitudes are eroding American morality.
iii. The network control of
     American TV is on the whole
     detrimental to the American
     viewer.

7.

Lee E. Staton is a student at Indiana University. He wrote to tell us of an unusual experience that happened there during his astronomy class:

Dear Mr. Roddenberry,
My astronomy professor and several
other professors at our Indiana University Southeast Branch are fans of <u>Star Trek</u>. Even though I had read that professors liked your show, I never quite
believed it until now.

As a practical joke during my astronomy large-group lecture, we slipped a film clip slide of the Enterprise into a set of slides the professor was showing of galactic nebulae, sunspots, clusters, etc. It was the most perfect set-up ever. Just as the professor shows us a Crab Nebula, he said, "There are a lot of weird things out there in space." Before he finished, the shot of the Enterprise went on the screen. The class broke into laughter and applause. And afterward he asked me for a copy of the slide, and I discovered his love for Star Trek.

                        Sincerely,
                        Lee E. Staton
                        Jeffersonville, IN

8.

Dr. Marvin R. Bensman is Associate Professor in the Department of Speech and Drama of Memphis State University. He teaches a course called "Radio-TV Programming." The description of the course in the Memphis State catalogue reads: "Analysis of individual program formats (with examples); use of this information along with ratings and other audience research to study the design of program schedules."

The books of Gerrold and Whitfield are again the course texts. Dr. Bensman draws heavily from STAR TREK in his course, and writes:

As you can tell, Star Trek is used primarily as a case-study since that is the only TV series, film, syndicated from network production which has been written about in such depth and from the exact angle which this course covers.

Also, students are fascinated by the series in itself and I am a science fiction fan from the age of seven.

9.

Julie Dickinson and Helen Wood taught a three-week interterm college course at Mt. Holyoke (Massachusetts) College in January, 1975. The psychology, sociology, anthropology, biology, chemistry, and physics brought out in the STAR TREK episodes were discussed. The course was a relaxed, informal seminar-type in which everyone discussed what they wished. Here is the three-week program:

Star Trek: The Phandom Phenomenon

First Week—Psychology of Star Trek
Believability of the show—Gene's "believability factor"
Why was it a good show/good science fiction
Why is there this fandom craze
Why was everybody taking the course

Second Week—Sociology-Anthropology
The Great Kirk Paradox
  Despite the prime directive, Kirk is continually deciding that a culture/society isn't the way it should be so he steps in and brings truth, justice and the American way.
  Question: Is Kirk justified in each case?
  "The Apple"
  "Taste of Armageddon"
  "A Private Little War"
  "A Piece of the Action"
  "Patterns of Force"
  "Friday's Child"

In "Is There in Truth No Beauty" everybody assumes Kollos is too _ugly_ (except Miranda)—why?

In "Galileo 7," burial is seen as important—even paramount—although the people who want to perform the burial might very well die during it.

In "Mark of Gideon" (Blish's version, and perhaps also in the show), Odonna says that the sick should be allowed to die; this shocks Kirk.

In "Conscience of the King," Kodos tried to save half of his people rather than have all of them die; afterwards, everyone tried to get him as a mass murderer.

In "Turnabout Intruder," women (as shown by Janice in Kirk's body) are seen as:
  constantly looking in a mirror
  being continually interested in their nails
  having hysterics when things go wrong,
and men never display any of these characteristics.

In "Is There in Truth No Beauty," it is assumed that just because Miranda is a human female, she will want the company of a human male someday. Why?

In "Patterns of Force," although the Nazi movement was started benevolently, it still turned out as 20th-century Earth Nazism did—is there perhaps some inherent flaw in the Nazi system, even when only the good parts are used?

In "Bread and Circuses," Kirk observes that advanced civilizations should not be worshipping the sun. Is this a valid statement?

In "Gamesters of Triskelion," "The Empath," and "The Menagerie," races of people had evolved quite far; however, none of the people felt emotion for anything or other peoples. Is this a natural consequence of evolution?

Third Week—Bio-physics, Chemistry

Spock is a hybrid, therefore H. sap. isn't a true species. They're not reproductively separate from Vulcans.

Consequences of Spock's hybridization, hybrid sterility, hybrid vigor.

Also on Spock—is he able to have sex all the time and only gets out of control every seventh year, or can he only function every seventh year? Consequences (physical and mental) of six years of celibacy.

Also, mentioned above that H. sap. and Vulcans not true species, yet both races had different origins (mentioned in "Return to Tomorrow").

In "All Our Yesterdays," the atavachron prepared the minds and bodies for living in the past. Once prepared couldn't leave that time, if not prepared couldn't live in that time; that species must have been evolving quite rapidly to make such preparations necessary; perhaps all of them are different species from each other.

How does faster-than-light travel affect time? Einstein's theory of relativity.

In "Alternative Factor," the two Lazaruses can never meet each other in one world because the meeting of the matter of one with the anti-matter of the other would destroy everything; is this consistent with what we know of electron-positron interaction?

Silicon life-forms suggested in "Devil in the Dark." Suitability of silicon as basis of life rather than carbon. Hybrid bonds: carbon vs. silicon. SiH_4 flammable in oxygen atmosphere.

Science behind: Dr. McCoy's instruments and sickbay, including the sterilite; transporter; warp drive; matter-antimatter engines; phaser; barrier at the edge of the galaxy.

Also during the course, the students were required to do a project. Projects could be doing almost anything creative related to <u>Star Trek.</u> One analyzed Federation foreign policy, several others invented aliens with biographies, planet histories, and careers in Star Fleet. Another made a stuffed mugato, one made a computer printout of the <u>Enterprise</u>'s silhouette, another drew a picture and wrote up a description for the home planet of the tribbles. Then when the course was over we had a mini-convention. The projects were set up, there was a trivia contest, films, people came in costume, and the entire community was invited.

10.

A professor from East Texas State University wrote to express his interest in STAR TREK as a teaching aid in mathematics:

August 25, 1975

Dear Mr. Roddenberry:

I teach mathematics here at E.T.S.U. and am teaching a leisure-learning course for non-credit this fall called "The Logic of Star Trek." I plan to discuss the logic that is used in some of the episodes to solve the problem at hand. At present we are planning to use the books by James Blish . . .

Mr. Prescott (of Filmation) suggested that I ask you for a Star Trek merchandise catalogue. I am also the sponsor of the Star Trek club on our campus and have a number of members that would like to have copies of such a catalogue. I wonder if you could send me 20 or so of them to pass out to the club members?

There seems to be quite a lot of interest around here in science fiction in general and Star Trek in particular. Many of us are going to the Con in Dallas in October and of course we are all eager to see the new movie about Star Trek that is upcoming.

Thank you very much for your help.

Sincerely yours,
Dr. John Lamb, Jr.
Associate Professor of Mathematics
East Texas State University
Commerce, TX

III

An interesting and certainly unusual use of STAR TREK in the learning process has been innovated by Edgar Rollins, who teaches at the Richmond, Virginia, City Jail. He wrote:

Greetings,

I am a teacher at the Richmond City Jail School. In the college-level psychology class conducted here with the inmates I use illustrations from <u>Star Trek</u> frequently to elaborate on course materials. An example. Human decision-making: the trinity of Kirk, Spock and McCoy representing this process. of course, Captain Kirk is the decision-maker. Mr. Spock represents (and is) logic, rationality, and information processing. Dr. McCoy is emotion, compassion, humanness, and intuition. The input of rationality and emotion to the decision-making process results in the responses to sets of stimuli, whether it be the <u>Enterprise</u> experiencing a crisis of galactic importance or the countless situations presented to us during the day. The input and weighing of emotion and logic and the appropriate response yield both success and wisdom for future events which we shall encounter.

In a broader sense the imagination presented and stimulated by <u>Star Trek</u> guides discussion in our classroom to the very nature and future of man-(etc.)-kind. It is a common ground on which we meet and explore. My behavior and attitudes and that of the inmate students are examined in all tenses, especially future.

Thank you for your contributions to the process.

                Continue!
                Edgar M. Rollins, Director
                Richmond City Jail School

John Cochran of the Department of Defense Computer Institute in Washington, D.C., teaches a short course using STAR TREK materials:

> I am the current course manager for the institute's "Requirements for Teleprocessing" course. This is a four-day course designed to educate students in data communications and its application to data processing. The nature of the course, dealing with a relatively new and dynamic field, lends itself toward the future. Therefore, an attempt is made to acquaint the students with today's and tomorrow's systems.
>
> The Star Trek slide that you sent us is used in a lecture entitled "Teleprocessing through 2000." Its purpose is to illustrate to students the future potential of computer/data communications systems.
>
> It is quite possible that some of the graphics showing the ship's interior display system, which you have generously agreed to send, will also be used in this same "future" lecture.
>
> Most sincerely,
> John J. Cochran
> Course Manager,
> Requirements For Teleprocessing
> Dept. of Defense Computer Institute
> Washington Navy Yard
> Washington, DC

Last summer, the Hackensack, New Jersey, Public Library sponsored a program for children that was both educational and fun. Children's Librarian Marilyn Olson wrote us about it:

> July 25, 1975
> Our summer reading club using Star Trek as a theme has proved remarkably

successful. Final statistics won't be in until the middle of September, but I fully expect that we will show a gain in both members and certificates awarded.

The basic feature of our club this year is the board that members move around on as they read books. There are twenty-five stops corresponding to how many books are read, except that we have counted by two's so that there is a maximum of 50. Each stop has an activity such as meeting the officers, visiting Sick Bay in the first half, and the second half is adventures such as meeting tribbles, visiting Planet Vulcan or encountering a magnetic storm. Several children are on their second and third trips around and we are only half-way through the summer. The purpose of the summer reading club is to encourage the children to read for pleasure at their present levels.

To a limited extent we have decorated the interior of the children's room to carry out this theme. Most of our materials are kept in a locked display case so that we will have them at the end of the summer. We have also made a special collection of science fiction available for borrowing, including, of course, all of the <u>Star Trek</u> books.

All staff members have been wearing buttons pertinent to the theme. They have elicited many comments and given us the opportunity to do advertising for the club.

Sincerely,
Marilyn Olson
Children's Librarian
Hackensack, NJ

The great variety of educational uses of STAR TREK as presented in this chapter, the overwhelming response of teachers to Janice Preston's branch of the Welcommittee, the knowledge that in some small way I myself am involved with this phenomenon that is having such a beneficial influence on the youth of our country—all these things make me extremely aware of my good fortune and add to my pride in being involved with STAR TREK. Janice Preston summed up the dedication of all those people in a letter to us:

> Is there any wonder that I have a special affection for Star Trek? Is there any wonder that I am fascinated by what it is bringing out in the schools, by what it is encouraging our aspiring scientists to achieve?

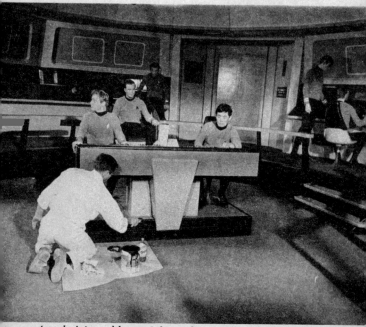

A technician adds a quick touch-up to the Bridge between takes.

Chapter Seven

The Big Screen

> My biggest wish is that I could be in a real <u>Star Trek</u> movie—even just walking down a corridor or sitting on the bridge.
> —*Thousands* of letters

In May of 1975 a tall, grinning man in his early fifties inserted a key into the door of Room 308 of Building E at Paramount Pictures. It was six long years since he had stood in this office. The furniture was different, but, as the man put it, the office gave him "good vibes." He talked about the carpeting. He had been responsible for its installation; likewise, the air-conditioning system and acoustic-tile ceiling in the executive office. He had his ice-making machine installed, and recalled the joyous cast and staff Christmas parties they'd had there. He indicated the special floor-to-ceiling bookcase/room-divider Matt Jefferies had designed. He sat in his oversized executive chair and stretched his long legs. It felt good to be back.

Gene Roddenberry had come "home" to do a STAR TREK movie.

After six years of hopes and frustrations, more hopes and more frustrations, Paramount Pictures had agreed to begin production of a motion-picture version of STAR TREK for theatrical release.*

Ironically, the only available offices were those he had occupied during the original STAR TREK television production.

Gene is not a man easily forgotten. Nearly everyone, from the studio guards to the plumbers, remembered him and welcomed him warmly, with an enthusiasm generally reserved for returning heroes.

---

* Although rumors are flying faster than warp eleven, no new television series, miniseries, or TV movies are being produced at this time. Current plans call for a film for theatrical distribution *only*.

THE BIG SCREEN 159

Gene Roddenberry and Matt Jefferies look at plans for the new movie.

"I can comment in sort of an amusing way on the reaction from people here at Paramount," says Gene. "It's divided into two main parts. The working people —the guards, the electricians, the people in the camera department and props and special effects— all of the people who actually *make* the pictures have just been marvelous. The first few weeks I could hardly walk down the street without people saying, 'Glad to have you back,' 'Wonderful!' 'Let's do great things again.' The crew or working-level people and I always got along fine. They knew we were trying to do something unusual, we had a challenge, they were a part of it, we all had fun, and our relationships were very good.

"Management relationships were somewhat different, and it came out of the fact that STAR TREK was an unusual bird. Here I was bringing in a spaceship with a pointy-eared hobgoblin as one of the people, going off to strange planets, rather Flash Gordon-ish, Buck Rogers-ish—and back in those days management really saw us in those terms.

"I had something else in mind. I wanted to do a show with the same care for quality, writing, and direction one would employ if he were doing a *Playhouse 90* or any of those great old shows. In order to make the show what I wanted to make it, I had to fight, and I had to fight very hard. Hardly a day went by that I was not involved in some confrontation with the people who spent the money, the people who assigned the stages, the network people and so on. I fought, and I won these fights by being very difficult. I knew I had to be difficult—*that* made STAR TREK what it was.

"However, three years of battling left some wounded egos and wounded feelings. I'm sure that many remember me as a difficult, touchy person. In many cases, they're right. Some of this I did purposely. I had a meeting with a studio executive who said, 'Gene, I'm going to give you some advice. You're beginning to get the nickname of "Crazy Gene" around the studio because you're calling up and saying how much does it cost to paint a woman green, stuff like that.' He said, 'The only way you can make the show what you want it to be is to take advantage of the fact that you *are* sort of a crazy person. Gene, actually you are fairly easy to get along with, but you've got to create the image of yourself as a battler, a fighter, a person who is liable to toss an executive out of your office if he comes in with an impossible request. This will do two things for you: one, a lot of them will not bother you on small items rather than fight with you. And the ones who do have a fight with you will recognize that they may lose when they go in. You've got to establish yourself as creative boss of STAR TREK.'

"And, following his advice, I did play a little bit of a role. Sometimes my anger or irritation was genuine, but quite as often it was role playing on my part. It left behind a lot of bruises. But if those bruises had not occurred, we would not have had the STAR TREK we know."

As this is being written, we've been at the studio now for seven months, and I've yet to see Gene live up to his reputation. Actually, I've *never* seen him lose his temper or even heard him raise his voice, though I suspect that the voice of a man of his imposing stature could boom like thunder if he so desired. When that happens, I think I'll go to lunch early!

Meanwhile, news of the planned movie spread like wildfire throughout fandom. Thousands of phone calls and truckloads of mail began swamping the studio. Everybody wanted to know about the movie. Everybody wanted to be *in* the movie! I doubt that there is a fan alive who would not give his entire STAR TREK collection to the Klingons in order to "just walk down a corridor"—that is, if he or she could wade through the crowds. (And Gene, who admits he dearly loves the fans, noted, "I wish they could!") We have a file full of applications from all over the country. Kids from everywhere are willing to quit school or leave their well-paying jobs just to come to Hollywood and be a "gopher" (go fer this, go fer that) on the set. They don't care what there is to do, how menial the task—they'll lick postage stamps, seal envelopes, dust desks, shine the shoes of stars, or anything else they can think of, just to be in on the Second Coming of STAR TREK. One lad wrote:

> I would like to know if you could use a 12-year-old that looks like a 16-year-old boy in any of your new movies or shows? I am enclosing a picture recently taken of myself, telephone number, address, height, weight, and measurements.
>
> I know you will refuse me and there is hardly any logic in asking (as Spock would put it!).
>
> I have a few blemishes and stuff, but after what you did to those ears, boy, you can do anything.
>
> I'm sure you could fit me in as Spock's or Jim's cousin, that I'm in trouble and Jim or Spock is the only one who can get me out of the trouble. I really have my hopes set on this.
>
> I'll have my fingers and toes crossed until you reply! And make the reply good!!!!

"We get a certain amount of mail of this type," says Gene, "that would be almost funny if it weren't for the pain you can read in some. I've gotten many letters from housewives—and some of them are rather middle-aged and, by our current standards of beauty, not particularly attractive people—who will pose in a bikini for a Polaroid shot, send it in, and say, 'Could you use me, my husband says I'm attractive!'

"And I'm sure such people are attractive in dimensions of caring, loving, and giving—gifts far beyond our two-dimensional television screen's power to convey."

The latest wave of mail now centers almost exclusively on the movie. Suspense and anxiety are continually building. As one fan wrote:

> Thank you for making the film, and please hurry. The waiting is horrible.

Frustrated by not knowing what the film will be about, and eager to fill the long, TREK-less months, the fans have again taken to their typewriters and have begun to send in their ideas and suggestions for the film. As noted in Chapter Eight, all unsolicited manuscripts have to be returned. But now and then, young fans send some intriguing and fun ideas along, with genuine sincerity. Beth Miller of Goshen, Indiana, had two requests:

> By the way, is there any way you could fit Roddy McDowall in? I love him, he's fantastic! He's already been in sci-fi. Give him a chance, Gene.

Perhaps she had in mind a kind of *Star Trek Meets Planet of the Apes,* something along the lines of the old *Frankenstein Meets Dracula* films. Her other suggestion was right to the point:

> Please get on TV. We have a yuckky theatre in town.

A fan in New York City, where theaters of every description abound, had these suggestions:

> Dear Mr. Roddenberry,
> When you make the <u>Star Trek</u> movie, please make it in "Sensurround" (you can feel the movie) and quadraphonic sound, and (if possible) "Smelly-O" (you can smell the movie). In the movie, try to

get in tribbles, Klingons, Romulans, and Spock's parents.

> Sincerely,
> Scott Palmieri

Other people have written and asked for Yeoman Rand, Lieutenant Kyle, T'Pring (Spock's fiancée), T'Pau (Vulcan's leader), Mariette Hartley, etc. One even suggested that Gene Roddenberry himself play a cameo role, à la Hitchcock. That's not a bad idea. Perhaps a scene with Gene dictating to his secretary . . .

Amy Foller, who suggested the cameo appearance, had some other very good ideas:

Dear Mr. Roddenberry,
I hope everything is progressing smoothly with your plans for the Star Trek movie and that Paramount executives are not giving you any trouble as they have in the past. I would now like to enumerate several suggestions and comments which you might find useful to consider while producing this film. I want to help because I care a great deal for Star Trek and everything and everyone behind it.

1) Undoubtedly you will want to improve the image of women on the Enterprise and in Federation society as well. One of the worst examples of how women were portrayed was in "Who Mourns for Adonais." In this episode Lt. Carolyn Palamas, who is supposed to be a competent archeologist and anthropologist, promptly forgets all of her training when she first catches sight of the handsome alien, Apollo. Only a lecture from the good captain keeps her from losing all touch with reality. Worse still is the way this affects Mr. Scott

(who was in love with her at the time), who is prompted to acts of blind fury, thus endangering himself as well as the others. It has been said that a chain is only as good as its weakest link. Therefore if Star Fleet was staffed with many Lt. Palamases it would surely fall apart without any help from the Romulans or the Klingons. Same for society.

Subpoint 1. One thing you might not have thought of that could do a great deal to improve the status of women in Star Fleet and the believability factor is to change the women's uniforms to pant uniforms like the men's. First the practical reasons: Pant uniforms are more realistic, in that starships visit planets with harsh climates and hostile weather conditions. Pants afford more protection from these elements and are better suited (pun not intended) for action purposes. On board ship they are more practical, especially for crawling under panels, working with corrosive material in science labs, and for working in the "Jefferies tube." On the sociopolitical side: the present mini-skirt uniforms make it clear to the women officers, (even Lt. Uhura) who <u>really</u> "wears the pants" on this starship.

Subpoint 2. Another element that would improve the image of women and Capt. Kirk as well as the idea of Kirk as a "cosmic womanizer." Mr. Gerrold mentions this in his book. However, it needs more emphasis. In practically every other episode some attractive (what other kind were there) female invariably tumbles into Kirk's arms. The cumulative effect is that (A) all women are helpless little things and need to be protected, and (B) this Capt. Kirk is very superficial in his relationships with women and does not regard them seriously. Also, the effect is that he is not a mature human being. Of course, we all know that Kirk is a dedicated Star Fleet officer and is therefore "married to his ship," so stories of this kind should not be told unless they are especially good, as in "City on the Edge of Forever."

2) Another thing you should consider is to convert all measurements to the metric system. <u>Star Trek</u> could be a great educational tool in helping Americans get acquainted with using this system of measurement. I groan inwardly every time I hear Mr. Spock (especially him) speak in terms of miles or inches rather than kilometers or centimeters. The metric system is the way of the future.

3) If you really enjoy challenges you might want to try to have some homosexually oriented crewmembers. Because if we can understand and tolerate other life forms and cultures, we can do the same for our own people who choose a different lifestyle.

I hope you have found my comments helpful or at least a little bit interesting. Please accept them in the spirit in which they were made. <u>Star Trek</u> is a wonderful thing with incredible vision and insight into the human experience. It is truly a nugget of gold in what Mr. Nimoy describes as "the bank of decent reality." Some people tell me that being a <u>Star Trek</u> enthusiast is "foolishness" or "kid stuff!" If so, I do not ever want to grow up. Continue striving for excellence in everything you do, Mr. Roddenberry, and I would consider it a rare privilege to help out in any manner that I am able.

>Yours in peace and friendship,
>Amy Foller
>San Carlos, CA

When kids write letters, they usually do so on school notebook paper, in the typical childlike scrawl. Such a letter arrived, hand-printed in huge block letters, from a very serious-minded youngster:

Dear Mr. Roddenberry,
This is a special business letter, and I have ideas for the introduction to your <u>Star</u> <u>Trek</u> movie.

I am 11 years old. Please do not think I'm crazy or something. I'm actually very serious. I will send you a tape of a theme that sounds pretty good.

I really must stop writing now. For additional info on it send a self-addressed stamped envelope to:

>Steve Lacy I
>Seabrook, TX

David Gerrold's tribbles, those prolific little balls of purring fur, are often requested:

You could have "tribbles" in one cage and Doctor McCoy could give them shots to keep them from getting pregnant . . . if you like my tribbles idea you could have someone slip them a shot of anti-whatever makes them pregnant and start the whole process over again.

An obvious Chekov fan wrote her ideas for a script:

David Gerrold (right) and Nichelle Nichols sign autographs at Vulcan II, held in New Orleans in May 1975.

Dear Gene Roddenberry,

How is your script coming? What is it going to be about? I am writing a <u>Star Trek</u> story which involves Lt. Uhura and Lt. Sulu. Do they have first names? If so, what are they? After all, it would sound dumb having good friends calling each other by their last names.

My story is about sort of a disease which makes the person who it affects do anything to kill the first person he sees after he gets it. I'm planning on having Scott get it, then Uhura, then Sulu, then Kirk and then Spock. That will put Chekov in command. I'm crazy about Chekov. Anyway, McCoy gets it, but realizes he has it and locks himself in his quarters before he sees anyone. In his quarters he figures a cure. Meanwhile, some danger is threatening the Enterprise (I haven't decided what) for Chekov to handle. Somehow McCoy cures himself and sets things to right. Chekov gets honors for his handling of the problems.

Yours,
Janette Kennedy
Sarasota, FL

Another fan also noticed that many of the characters do not have first names. One fan, the president of his local fan club, wrote:

Mr. Roddenberry,
While reading The World of STAR TREK I found a serious fault in Vulcan logic. The fault is this: Why only one name? Why haven't they developed second names like Earthmen have? Not having second names is illogical. Think of the poor clerk in the Vulcan hall of records!

A loyal fan,
Larry Sommers

Many fans, concerned that the original cast would not be back (we are hopeful that they will *all* be in the film), and that the studio had been having difficulty finding a proper script, have expressed their dismay on both counts. April Pentland (who, you may recall, had another comment in Chapter Five) expressed her ideas on this subject:

August 28, 1975

Dear Mr. Roddenberry,
News services leak the discouraging

information that vital members of the original cast are now involved with new series. Most recent inquiries into the status of the proposed movie reveal that production has not progressed beyond requests for script outlines. This report I find hard to believe. With such prestigious writers as Harlan Ellison, Theodore Sturgeon and Norman Spinrad contributing scripts for the original series, and classic episodes created by D. C. Fontana, not to mention the driving force of your own creative genius, I would not think there would be any shortage of ideas. Of course, a movie for theatrical release is more demanding than one episode of a continuing series. It must stand contained in itself, without preceding or following episodes in which further delineation of characters or circumstances can be drawn. This consideration must be made even though the majority of the audience will be thoroughly familiar with both. But the wealth of current science fiction writers who could create, or adapt vital, thoughtful, compelling, mind-stretching adventures for the Enterprise is almost too great to make one choice possible. Writers who deal with the power and potential of humanity, rather than with gadgetry or bug-eyed monsters: Arthur C. Clarke, Frank Herbert, Ursula LeGuin, Larry Niven, Poul Anderson, Theodore Sturgeon, most especially and magically Roger Zelazny, or even Robert Heinlein if you're desperate. If the fans and followers of science fiction are dynamic, involved, positive individuals, as proven by the existence of the conventions, the fanzines, and letters like this one, enough to overload the computers at NBC, can the creators of science fiction be any less? I simply refuse to believe that <u>Star Trek</u> can be stalled by any poverty of imagination.

But if, in fact, the glory cannot be recaptured, if the stellar forces you brought together for three years of blindingly brilliant, heart-stirring exploration of the depth and breadth of the human spirit cannot be recalled from their new orbits, then all I can say is thank you. For those of us you have touched, the hope of the <u>Enterprise</u> will never die, long after the last "Beam Me Up" T-shirt has been torn up for dust cloths. It was a glimpse of Camelot. Not the magically ordained and ordered fairy tale of antediluvian perfection, but the real and tangible proof that man can attain that in which he truly believes. That we are not victims. That Captain Kirk, as commander of a starship, and you, as producer of a television series, can know, learn, understand, and deal with all the pressures, all the unknowns, all the problems, and create and accomplish something lasting and valuable.

<u>We</u> <u>are</u> <u>not</u> <u>victims</u>! It is a message that cries for reaffirmation. Today, when the government that controls so much of our lives is more of a mystery to us than the orbits of distant stars. We are not helpless. We are not ineffectual. We are not merely functioning statistics in the G.N.P. We will not be paralyzed by the weight of our own inertia. We are not alone. The spirit of

the Enterprise will always endure for me, but I pray that for all the millions you have touched it will also become a phoenix. The message of hope, of optimism, may be an eternal truth, but it is pathetically easy to forget that truth in the world today. We need to be reminded that one man with an ideal he believes in can make the dream a reality. We need your courage, and James Kirk's, his idealism and capacity for love. We need Spock's sanity, and McCoy's iconoclastic humor, and Scotty's fanatic sense of human responsibility. Thank you for that glimpse of Camelot. I fervently hope that you, and we, will find it again.

Live long and prosper,
April Pentland
Auburn, MA

STAR TREK provides a healthy outlet for young dreamers who enjoy fantasizing about what it would be like to live in the STAR TREK future (and, let's face it, we've all thought about it). Often we get letters from would-be lovers of Captain Kirk, Spock, Chekov, etc. Male writers are all madly in love with Nurse Chapel (Majel Barrett admits these are her favorite letters!) or Uhura. Many young writers like to imagine that they are related to various crew members, and would naturally be in a STAR TREK episode of the future. The movie (and potential spin-offs) lends itself to these ideas most readily. One young teenager wrote, somewhat wistfully:

Dear Gene Roddenberry,
My name is Donnaray Crouch and I'm 14 years old. I'm writing to you about an idea I've come up with for a new Star Trek series. This is the idea:

This show would be similar to the previous series, but taking Mr. Spock's place would be a young girl Vulcan (myself) who would be Mr. Spock's younger sister. Because she was born late in her parents' life, unlike Earth people, who are sometimes handicapped after birth, she would be a genius and child prodigy, even for a Vulcan. The young girl would be unemotional like Mr. Spock, but instead of black hair she would have light brown hair. This young girl would be the only child on ship except maybe for some episodes with other kids as guest stars.

The reason I've come up with this idea and am submitting it to you is to give me a chance to fulfill my desire to appear on T.V. I do not have an agent but am interested in obtaining one. Enclosed is a drawing of me and how I'd look as Mr. Spock's sister.

> Thank you,
> Donnaray Crouch
> Milpitas, CA

Some *very* original suggestions were submitted by other young people. One sent in this interesting, if somewhat gory, idea:

I have a small suggestion (I know you get millions of them!) for your Star Trek movie. I know in past episodes blood has rarely been shown, but in the movie if there are any scenes where someone bleeds, I think it would look good if it were Spock. For instance, say Spock's arm is cut, imagine the reaction when green blood spurts out? See what I mean?

> Brian Deslatte
> Port Neches, TX

While you're pondering that, here's what a boy from Virginia offered:

```
Dear Mr. Roddenberry,
   Here are a few ideas and thoughts you
might be able to use in Star Trek:
   1. Because the crew of the Enterprise
live in an artificial atmosphere, they
would need sun lamps to stay healthy.
   2. In Sick Bay why not add a dentist,
and maybe a ship head shrink.
   3. How about some pockets.
   4. A telephone for the married members
of the crew to call home, when near
enough.
   5. And in case some crew members get
stuck on an ice-age planet, because of
transporter malfunction, a long rope and
a pot of hot coffee.
   I hope that the above are useful.
                        Peace and long life,
                        John R. Guthrie III
                        Radford, VA
```

Now that we've heard the fans' ideas on the movie, what does Gene Roddenberry hope the film will be?

"I want it to be more than just an elongated STAR TREK television episode," he says. "I don't want to go out and fight the Klingons again. Because this is a motion picture, it takes a slightly different form, and we're going to try to bring people into the theater who, even though they're not STAR TREK fans, will still like the show. But at the same time, it's sort of a narrow line to walk. I don't want to change the essential format of the show, or the essential characters, if only for the professional economic reason that they have worked and worked well. Why discard things that do work well?"

In a letter addressed "Paramount Pictures, Hollywood, Calif."* Brent J. Farlie expressed very simply what to him obviously needs to be done:

```
Dear Sirs:
  I have recently heard that you are
working on a screenplay for a Star Trek
film. The only thing that I could sug-
gest to you is, get Gene Roddenberry,
the original cast, and do it!
                Brent J. Farlie
                Supervisor,
                  Western Regional Office
                Dempster Dumpster Systems
                Sunnyvale, CA
```

And so, hopefully, they will do just that.

---

* All mail not addressed to anyone's specific attention is handled by the studio publicity department, according to studio policy. They sort it, but keep no count. It is then forwarded to our office, to do with as we see fit.

Preparing for a take in D. C. Fontana's "The Enterprise Incident" are Joanne Linville as the Romulan commander and Leonard Nimoy as Mr. Spock.

Chapter Eight

Who, What, Where, When, Why, and How Come?

```
Mr. Spock, could you please
come to my house for dinner?
                —Seven-year-old boy
```

If there is one thing all STAR TREK followers seem to have in common, it is their ability to think up challenging questions about the series, about fandom, and about the STAR TREK mystique. STAR TREK fans want to know *everything* about STAR TREK, and they're not afraid to ask!

> Can you tell me why Spock's mother wears a gown or dress that shows her underclothes?

Maybe she's trying to get herself a fanzine centerfold too.

> Is Captain Kirk's favorite sandwich chicken salad, or unstated?

He prefers unstated, on rye, hold the mayo.

> I would like to know <u>Star Trek's</u> birthday.

STAR TREK is a Virgo, born September 8, 1966, when the NBC network first gave birth to a bouncing sixty-minute television program.

> I would like to know if the following have been invented: a stun ray force field, tricorder, dematerializing ray, tractor beam, deflector shield, deflector beam, transporter device, disruptor

beam, universal translator, laser gun, ray that kills but doesn't burn (like phaser gun set on "kill"), a device that can emit different rays (like a phaser gun), matter and anti-matter engine, turbo-elevator, computerized robot (that walks and talks), and an android.

Mostly no. Good luck!

These, of course, are not the commonly asked questions. They are a good deal of fun and show imagination and careful attention to details. Most of the questions we receive are serious, and quite frequently appear in letter after letter. We usually reply to these

Susan Sackett opening letters to Star Trek *in her office at Paramount Studios.*

questions with form letters, not because of laziness or indifference, but because our office would accomplish very little else if we answered each question individually. *Here are the most frequently asked questions:*

How may I rent a copy of a <u>Star Trek</u> episode, or the blooper reel?

Sorry, neither STAR TREK episodes nor the Blooper Reel are available for rental to individuals. Conventions and educational institutions should contact Paramount's Legal Department for further information on episodes.

Here is a script I wrote. Can you please consider it for <u>Star Trek</u>?

Sorry, studio regulations prohibit Gene from accepting or even looking at any manuscript, story, or series idea unless it is submitted through a recognized literary agent. *All unsolicited manuscripts are returned unread.*

Where can I write to my favorite <u>Star Trek</u> actor/actress?

The best way to reach them is to send mail in care of their individual fan-club presidents. (See Appendix for addresses.) *Do not write* and ask us for home addresses, telephone numbers, and so on. It's also best not to hold your breath waiting for William Shatner to dance with you at your prom, or for Leonard Nimoy to share your mom's spaghetti at your house. Which reminds me of one of the most charming letters ever, in *huge* childish handwriting:

Dear Star Trek:
 I am Sheila Dawn Boyer. My sister wants Doctor McCoy to come over to our house. Here is the house number . . .
P.S. I love you. Please come over. If

you can't come over then send Kirk. If he can't come over then write me lots of notes. P.P.S. I am eight.

For the record: Dr. McCoy never makes house calls!

What ever happened to Grace Lee Whitney?

Ms. Whitney, who played the part of Yeoman Janice Rand in the first season of STAR TREK, says that her part was written out in the second and third seasons so that Captain Kirk could have other romantic interests. Fans still remember her, and she is very fond of her STAR TREK friends, too. She plans to attend some of the conventions and now has her own fan club (see Appendix).

Grace Lee has done numerous television guest appearances on such shows as *Walt Disney, Gunsmoke,*

Grace Lee Whitney sans Yeoman Rand makeup.

Grace Lee Whitney today.

Bonanza, Mannix, Cannon, Mod Squad, Bewitched, and *The Bold Ones*. She was a regular on *Khan*, a recent, short-lived CBS entry.

A native of Detroit, Grace Lee is currently appearing in various nightclubs around Los Angeles with a singing group, and admits that her first love is singing. She's married to composer Jack Dale (he writes all her material) and has two teenage boys from a previous marriage (as small children they appeared in the STAR TREK episode "Miri"), plus two stepchildren—both teenage girls—five Great Danes, and a houseful of lovely green plants. Her long, platinum-blond hair now falls to her waist. She keeps her slim figure and youthful appearance by working out daily in a gym and eating health foods. She hasn't aged a bit since her "Yeoman Rand" days. And, oh yes, she has her own airplane—christened *Star Trek II*.

When is there going to be a convention in my area?

Probably soon. Conventions are quite frequent occurrences lately, each "Con" spawning numerous others. For information on the next one, write to the STAR TREK Welcommittee; send one dollar plus a *self-addressed, stamped envelope* to: Allyson Whitfield, STW Directory, P.O. Box 206, New Rochelle, NY. The directory also has information on more than two hundred fan clubs.

I want to sell some Star Trek items. How do I get a license?

If your club is doing this for its own support and the sale is not a profit-making venture, chances are you won't need one. Check with Paramount's Legal Department. Those wishing to sell a product *for profit* should write to Mr. Lou Mindling, c/o Paramount Pictures, 5451 Marathon St., Hollywood, CA 90038.

Where can I buy phasers/communicators/tricorders/models etc.?

Most of this "hardware" is available in model kits from toy or hobby stores.

Where can I get Lincoln's current catalogue?

Send a business-sized *self-addressed, stamped envelope* to: Lincoln Enterprises, P.O. Box 38429, Hollywood, CA 90038. No letter is necessary; they'll send you the free catalogue. *NO* C.O.D. orders, please!

Where can I get the <u>Star Trek Concordance</u>?

Bjo Trimble has reedited and combined her concordances into a single volume covering both the original three seasons and all of the animated shows. Published by Ballantine Books, *The Star Trek Concordance* is available for $6.95 at your local bookstore or from Ballantine Cash Sales, P.O. Box 505, Westminster, Maryland 21157 (Please add 50¢ for postage and handling; allow four weeks for delivery).

And some questions about the movie:

What is the status of the movie?

Please don't call our office for this information. It only hinders the progress of the movie, and none of us wants that to happen. The best source of information is *STAR TREKTENNIAL NEWS*, published six times a year by Lincoln Enterprises ($7.50 a year). This is the newsletter of the *official* International STAR TREK Fan Club. As editor of STN, I maintain a close watch on all movie activities from my office at the studio, and report accurate, up-to-the-minute happenings in each issue.

Will I be able to visit the set of the movie?

The Paramount lot is a "closed-set" studio and does not carry insurance to cover visitors.

I would like to be on the staff/in the cast of the movie.

So would just about every fan! Unfortunately, there are only so many jobs, and most studio jobs are filled with union members. We all want this to be the finest motion picture possible; naturally, Gene is going to hire the most experienced staff he can! Casting, on the other hand, is done by a *casting director,* who is in constant touch with the various talent agencies in the Hollywood area. If you have such aspirations, get yourself an agent and have *him* contact us.

Will the original cast be used?

Yes, if they are not involved at the time in another series and do not have conflicting commitments.

Will there be new props, sets, and costumes in the movie?

Yes. None of the old sets, props, or costumes remain. The *Enterprise* will be given a "face lift," but she'll still be quite recognizable.

Will there be a new <u>Star Trek</u> television series?

We have no plans for one at this time. However, a miniseries is a possibility if the movie should prove successful.

Now and then we get a serious letter from a fan who hopes to be a director, writer or producer. Gene answered one inquiry on directing this way:

The first thing you must do is prepare for college, where you can major in cinema or theater arts, by getting involved in the stage productions at your own high school. There are a number of paperback books and magazines which deal with film direction, and your local library or paperback dealer should be able to provide them for you.

Spend as much time as possible watching film for construction, camera work, interaction of people. If you have access to an 8-mm camera, use it to begin experimenting with your own films. Directing, as with any other art or craft, demands long years of study and preparation. No one really just walks in and becomes a director. While you are in school, devote all the time you can to school productions and then go on to college, where you will be involved in making films. After college, (you must have a B.A.) you can apply to the Directors Guild of America as a candidate for their apprentice program. This is a difficult program to "crack," but it is well worthwhile if you make it.

Later on, when you are old enough to work on a summer job, you might apply to the local television station if there is one nearby. Even if you are only employed in the mail room, there is the opportunity to learn.

As I said before, it is not easy, and it does not happen overnight. You must be prepared to work long and hard at learning and developing your art.

Another question Gene is asked frequently is "How

does science fiction differ from fantasy?" Here is one way he expressed the difference in a letter to a fan:

> Science fiction differs from fantasy by involving itself in extrapolations of present knowledge and generally staying true to physical laws as we understand them at present. Science fiction can also be an extrapolation of <u>conditions</u> as we know them now, that is, social, religious, economic, etc. It can be a contemporary story or go backward or forward in time.
>
> The science-fiction author can change physical laws or facts, i.e., he can postulate that women are an alien race and only seem to have been born here on this planet (or maybe he's right), or he can invent something totally new and unsuspected as long as it stays true to the universe as we understand it. Or he can pretend that some certain shift in physical laws has occurred. Important— once he has done any of these things, he must remain absolutely true to his hypothesis throughout the story. There are probably other conditions and exceptions too, but these occur to me most immediately. In other words, science-fiction stories exist in an <u>ordered</u> universe where even new inventions and new hypotheses stay true to the order.
>
> Fantasy, on the other hand, need abide by no recognized rules. Its features need not be derived from anything we know at all, and it can easily come out of superstition, mythology and so on. An example of fantasy which looks like science fiction would be Blackbeard and a pirate crew armed with cutlasses trav-

Gene Roddenberry at work in his office at Paramount Studios.

eling in a rocket vessel which uses solid ball cannon to capture other spacecraft. Any culture capable of space travel has already achieved a science far beyond cutlasses and cannon as offensive weapons. About the only thing which could conceivably make the preceding example science fiction would be making a story point that some religion or ceremonial usage of the culture prohibits any other kind of weapon, a prohibition so strong that even pirates follow it.

Gene says that the question most often asked about STAR TREK is: "Why the incredible support of its fans?" Some of the reasons have already been discussed (in Chapter One). In his college lectures, he often tries to answer that question, but finds it still somewhat of a mystery. "I wish I knew all of the answers to that," says Gene. "For myself, for the remarkable cast, production staff, and crew who somehow came together during those bruising, exhausting, completely lovely years . . . it *was* an effort to prove something about the television audience. We believed that people were not only willing, but anxious to think beyond the petty beliefs that have for so long kept humanity divided. We used to say that we suspected there was an intelligent life form on the other side of the television tube, and we planned to use our show to signal some of our thoughts to them. But I do not expect or consider STAR TREK to be all things to all people. I consider it to be far from a perfect television show. But it was one thing—for all of us involved, it was a hell of a lot of fun to make."

Chapter Nine

Dreams for a Future

I believe a real-life Federation
can be built by 1985. . . .
please give me a small donation,
say $25.

—California youth

"Space . . . the final frontier . . ."

The familiar voice-over, the lingering starscape, the feeling of imminent excitement—and we are armchair astronauts off on another STAR TREK adventure.

Many fans not only saw the *Enterprise*'s voyages as an adventure, but as a future reality. A question that is very often asked of Gene Roddenberry is "Do you really see STAR TREK as an accurate depiction of what you expect the future to be like?" His answer is always definite: "No. Only in the sense that we do have an exciting future ahead of us. But in order to sell the show, and keep it on the air in front of a twentieth-century mass audience, I had to people it with twentieth-century men and women who were depicting twentieth-century problems and values.

"I think the next two hundred to three hundred years will see great changes in the species, great changes in values and attitudes and so on. For example, I doubt that the institution of marriage as we presently know it will survive another half century . . . I think that certainly people of different sexes or the same sex will find those with whom they feel comfortable, whose attitudes give pleasure and strength to the other, and they will have relationships, sexual and nonsexual. But I doubt very much that it will be a marriage contract. I think that by a half century from now there will be a thing like 'children's liberation.' I think for people to own their children as they do today is rather primitive. To own a child, I think, is as unfair and destructive as the old system in which a man owned his wife and could chastise her, beat her, or punish her. Today we accept that you can own your children, and you can chastise and beat them. Very wise people, maybe, can handle this, but I think it's quite obvious that many people aren't up to the responsibility. I hope we will reach a time when every child is everyone else's child, that any child is looked on by all adults as one of the most precious resources of humankind, and children's training and upbringing will not be the hit-or-miss family thing that we have now.

"I am not a communist, but at the same time, I think the idea of a person or corporation owning hunks of our resources has got to go. I think our political systems have got to change or are going to be changed enormously. I think our system of high materialism, our system of advertising, is largely an institution of deceit and greed. Unfortunately, in making STAR TREK, I was dealing with twentieth-century minds that accept these things. 'Motherhood is next to Godliness,' and 'The most important thing for my daughter is to marry an accountant.' If I had presented my ideas to our audience unadulterated, I would have been lucky to play to a million people, much less to the eighteen million we needed to stay on the air. In fact, I never would have gotten it through a network office. It would have been greeted like a combination of blasphemy, communism, anarchy, and insanity. There is no way STAR TREK could reflect where I think we're going."

Gene does believe, however, that we are headed for a well-developed space-exploration program, and hopes that STAR TREK may have an effect on the voters and on our young generation today, who will vote to fund future space programs, whose enthusiasm will make them possible. We've had letters from several of these people who have taken STAR TREK's version of the future to heart. One young lad wrote the following proposal:

March 24, 1975

Dear Gene Roddenberry,

I believe a real-life Federation can be built by 1985 and a Space Academy built by early 1979. The Federation consists of building a starship, the parts on Earth, and shipping them up in N.A.S.A.'s shuttlecrafts.

I'm going to put the Space Federation initiative on the November '76 ballot of all 50 states. I need $20,000 to do that: $10,000 goes to the attorney generals and $10,000 goes for correspondence to all American colleges of the U.S.A., and advertisement. Five hundred thousand (500,000) signatures are required for California's ballot and there are 300,000 students in California so I think we'll get it.

You think NBC can donate or loan the money? I'm sure some states will pass it and NBC will be paid back. I need $20,000. Please ask them.

By 1985, 432 specially trained crewmen, half are women, will take off for Alpha Centauri.

So please help, Gene. You please give me a small donation, say $25, so I can correspond with the California colleges.

This is not a zonk project. I've been working on the Federation since October '73. The ship will look like the starship on your show and it will be 1017 feet long.

I'll need William Shatner as Captain Kirk to do advertisements introducing the Space Federation.

Thank you,
Kip Lee
Redding, CA

One young boy had plans to build only the starship *Enterprise:*

Dear Gene,
 I just love your show, and I've got great news for you. I am going to create a real starship Enterprise. I've got it all planned out. Here's my plan: I am going to earn as much money as I can and when I get about $7,000 I will go to the rocket factory and ask them if they would help me build a starship Enterprise. If they do, they can be part of my crew, and you can be my First Officer. Oh, by the way, would you send me some maps and drawings of the starship Enterprise? And please send me a picture of the bridge too.

Love,
Greg Pharr
Austin, TX

And should the *Enterprise* have trouble getting off the ground, here is what another boy suggested:

My "golden dream"—that is to make an exact replica of the Enterprise and turn it into a hotel. I estimate the cost at 80 million dollars and 40 years to pay off. I admit it's a long time to pay off, but I'd live in it for free. Truly my dream come true.

Sincerely,
Roy Cameron Walker
Memphis, TN

Other fans are content to dream about being a part of the crew, traveling on the *Enterprise* to distant star systems:

When the _Enterprise_ goes to Orion or Beta Antares 7, you're really there. It's really happening, it's great!

April 25, 1975

Dear Star Trek,

My friend Chuck and I like to pretend that we are a part of the _Star Trek_ crew and we make up our own little fun by doing some acts where we live. Most of the people around there call us crazy because we do this, but they don't know what it means to us. We use our own gadgets to have them similar to yours. We use our tape recorder as a tricorder, our walkie-talkies as the communicators, and fire cracker guns as phasers. We live in the woods and near a sawmill, and we use the woods as an unexplored planet that we beamed down on. We use the sawmill as the headquarters of the aliens of this planet.

John Wilson
Lebanon, PA

One fan wrote a prayer for future space travelers:

An Old Federation Saying

May the warp drive always be at your
   back,
Your phasers always fully charged,
Your deflector shields always up,
And may the star date on which
You transport out of this life
And into the next
Be a long time.

Butch Hoover
Edmond, OK

If STAR TREK is having an impact on the youngsters, it has also had quite an effect on our world today. Many of STAR TREK's ideas of future inventions have already become a part of our every day living. One example is the "beeper" or pulse sound on Dr. McCoy's monitors. A Vermont nurse wrote to tell us of its current hospital usage:

> The pulse sound of Dr. McCoy's monitors has been used as a life-saver in real hospital situations. Several different models of oscilloscopes (monitors) with varying sounds are available. Their common and main function is to allow doctors and nurses to be aware of any change in cardiac (heart) rhythm. Each pulse beat causes a "beep." A change in rates or rhythms, as shown both by the sounds and by the "picture" on the screen, may mean a critical change in the patient's condition, requiring immediate corrective measures. The rate, rhythm, and screen changes may also show the effectiveness of past medicines and treatments. Naturally, many false alarms occur, as well as many normal changes. However, our monitors have never failed to show a life-threatening problem.
>
> Nurses familiar to the special care unit (combined coronary and intensive care) have learned to listen for any change in "beep" sounds, as well as learning to read the monitor screen's picture.
>
> Another area where <u>Star Trek</u> and the hospital are closely allied is in a type of metal syringe holder we use for "shots." A glass tube, prefilled with medicine, and with needle preattached,

is inserted into the metal "Tubex" holder. Many different meds can be given to a variety of patients, using the same holder, merely by changing glass tubes. Each glass medicine tube and needle is only used once. The "Tubex" holders are almost shaped like Dr. McCoy's air hypo holders.

This metal holder is very frightening to both children and adults, due to its size, but children are especially frightened by it. Many times I have helped reduce a child's fear by showing them the "Tubex" without the needle, letting them examine it, and then comparing it to Dr. McCoy's air hypo. The mention of Star Trek and Dr. McCoy has an almost magical effect on children. We do occasionally have children in the special care unit, and anything which helps them adjust to a truly terrifying environment is of great benefit.

                Sincerely yours
                Barbara L. Cook, R.N.
                Brattleboro, VT

Some branches of the United States government have expressed interest in various aspects of STAR TREK. When the Smithsonian Institution opened its new National Air and Space Museum in 1976, STAR TREK was there:

                Sept. 24, 1975
Dear Ms. Sackett:
In response to your letter of 14 September we are pleased to tell you of our interest in Star Trek.

It all started in August 1967 when Gene Roddenberry offered, and the museum accepted, a print of the Star Trek pilot film, #2, "Where No Man Has Gone Before." This film is in a protected archive and not available for public screening.

We believe that science fiction can play a "mind-stretching" role in the minds of creative, scientific and technically inclined persons. All three of the acknowledged rocket pioneers, Tsiolkovsky, Goddard and Oberth, acknowledged the influence of Jules Verne. In addition, Goddard had high interest in H. G. Wells' First Men on the Moon. The large number of scientific and technical professionals who indulge in speculative fiction today reinforces this view: motion pictures, e.g., "2001: A Space Odyssey," and the Star Trek series represent the same kind of invitation to imaginative thinking as books but in different genre.

As plans for our new museum building developed we inquired of possible artifacts available from the Star Trek production sets, the program having been terminated. Matt Jefferies has donated the Klingon battle cruiser model (about 30 inches long) and a 4-inch block of plastic containing a tiny model of the Enterprise used in the episode "Catspaw." David Gerrold has given us a few tribbles.

Paramount has donated the large (11½-foot long) studio model of the Enterprise to the museum. Received in early 1974, it was in several pieces and in deteriorated condition. A few parts were missing. We performed some cosmetic restoration and displayed the model from mid-September 1974 to January this year in our _Life in the Universe_ exhibit. Franz Joseph's blueprints of the interior were exhibited nearby.

We have moved to our new building and are developing exhibits preparatory to our opening 4 July 1976. The new museum is a major structure on the Mall here in Washington. It is located at 600 Independence Avenue, S.W. The sweeping story of flight from earliest times to possible space exploration will be shown in twenty-four exhibit galleries. When we open, the _Enterprise_ will be fully refurbished and re-wired for lighting. It will be exhibited in the _Life in the Universe_ gallery.

Besides Gene Roddenberry and Matt Jefferies, we have enjoyed the assistance and cooperation of Dorothy Fontana and Bjo Trimble as well as many others in developing a reference file of scripts, fan magazines, etc. on the _Star Trek_ phenomenon.

This is a quick view and report on the Smithsonian's interest in the subject. We are limited in the time we can give to the subject but recognize high interest on the part of a sizable number of our visiting public.

With all good wishes,

        Sincerely,
        F. C. Durant, III
        Assistant Director
        Astronautics
        Smithsonian Institution
        Washington, DC

Richard C. Hoagland is Science Advisor to NASA. When he heard that Gene would possibly be writing a STAR TREK motion picture, he immediately offered

The world's largest solar telescope at the Kitt Peak National Observatory, Tucson, Arizona, forms the backdrop for the presentation of a Flight Deck Certificate to Richard C. Hoagland (left) by Gene Roddenberry. Mr. Hoagland is science advisor to NASA.

some personal advice, ideas, and thoughts on the future and how STAR TREK might best present that future:

April 2, 1975

Dear Gene,

Every age seems to have thought of itself as unique in history. Someone sooner or later always pulls out that chestnut about things going to the dogs and kids having no respect for their parents, only to drop the punchline that the quote is from Plato. However, that not withstanding, this point in history _is_ unprecedented. It is the first time that the free spirit of men has met apparently inviolable limits. Mankind has outgrown the limitations of Earth, in its ability to supply both its material needs and, more importantly, its spiritual necessities. Men have never done well when placed under artificial limitations. The experience in Eden proved that. Now, we are told that the future is not only going to be different from the past (something only recently accepted by most people), we are happily informed that it will be worse—many more to take care of and less to go around. The Mid-East is only a foretaste of what is to come, if this philosophy prevails, as increasing billions with rising expectations crowd onto a depleted world and take out their frustrations on those who arrived first and made it, so to speak . . .

It is against this dismal picture that one Gene Roddenberry created a vision of the future that apparently has caught the imagination of an awful lot of people, from all ages and cultural backgrounds. It is a vision of people from many parts of the galaxy, cooperating, meeting adventure and adversity with a can-do spirit, and enjoying the experience. It has caused an unprecedented phenomenon in mass media. It is an island of hope in a dark sea of growing despair. And now, that island is about to become a continent, with the production of the first feature-length <u>Star Trek</u> epic. That's right, I said epic. Because that is what we need.

What we lack today in every area of human endeavor is leadership. We have no heroes, no idols, no one we look up to anymore. We have met our Watergate and it may have killed our inner selves. Or did John Kennedy's death do it?

The result is that we are a ship of state without a captain. The bridge is empty and we are headed for the reefs.

Therefore, at the risk of offending the creative artist, I'm going to express a few hopes and fears vis-à-vis this forthcoming epic, for it should be precisely that. The audience, now spanning at least two generations, which has been caught up in the spirit of a rather exceptional TV serial, now expects something <u>very</u> exceptional from the feature film. They need it.

As you well know it is the arts which most reflect the temper of a culture. But occasionally, just occasionally, it is an art form which must lead a society to a new level of consciousness. And that is my hope for your feature-length <u>Star Trek</u>. In a time of leaderless confusion, about who we are, about our apparent "failure in success," and about where we are going, this film could be a ray of desperately needed hope. And what is critically important—<u>it will be listened to</u>.

I'm not talking about any specific story, or plot. That, certainly, is your prerogative as a writer. But you have created a universe as real to millions of people as the one we inhabit, day to day. That universe was built on careful attention to detail and consistency. It is my strong recommendation that that kind of careful planning in background be used to illustrate a possible solution to today's crises, while at the same time filling in some of the gaps between the present and the Star Trek era 200 years hence. People need to see that their problems have solutions that history is not drawing to a close, but just beginning. Somehow, that should be conveyed by what you will do . . .

It is a fascinating coincidence that the Star Trek universe should be set approximately 200 years from now. In my role as advisor to the N.A.S.A. Bicentennial Committee, I have suggested several projects on the theme, "the next 200 years." . . .

It seems to me, therefore, quite appropriate that the release date of the Star Trek feature will be semi-coincident with the start of these celebrations of our heritage, part of which some of us are trying valiantly to get aimed toward the idea, "where do we go from here?" . . .

You have their attention, Gene. Tell them something important.

        Enviously,
        Dick Hoagland
        Science Advisor to N.A.S.A.
        Goddard Space Flight Center
        Greenbelt, MD

In August, 1975, a STAR TREK convention to end all conventions was held in Chicago. It received national attention, and its financial success was even reported in *The Wall Street Journal*. One of the invited speakers at the convention was Jesco von Puttkamer, a NASA representative working on long-range plans for manned space flight. He wrote to Gene of his experiences at the Chicago Con:

> National Aeronautics and
> Space Administration
> Washington, DC 20546
> 26 August, 1975
>
> Mr. Gene Roddenberry
> Star Trek
> 5451 Marathon Street
> Hollywood, CA 90038
>
> Dear Mr. Roddenberry:
>
> Our mutual friend, Fred Durant, was kind enough to mention my then-planned presentations at the Chicago Star Trek Convention in his letter to you of 8/12. He also passed on to me your reply. I, also, regretted it that you were unable to attend.
>
> I enjoyed the Convention and expect that N.A.S.A. will continue supporting these efforts; some personal observations that may interest you are enclosed. Both the fans and your very loyal "Enterprise crew" made sure I fully understood that with your absence the most important Star Trek factor was missing.
>
> Since it is my job in the Office of Manned Space Flight to lead our field centers at Huntsville, Houston, and Cape Canaveral in trying to develop a long-range integrated plan for manned space flight, I am interested in how the "outside" world sees the future. Conversely, we are also interested in having the

public see what we are thinking in advanced planning. Some of this is summed up in the two enclosed papers, which you may find of interest.

I certainly would like very much to meet with you as Fred suggested. Maybe there will be a chance sometime. In the meantime, if I can be of any help to you, please feel free to contact me.

>With best wishes,
>Jesco von Puttkamer
>Advanced Programs, Code MTE
>Office of Manned Space Flight

Mr. von Puttkamer was kind enough to enclose his Convention Report to NASA:

Memorandum
To: F/John P. Donnelly
From: MTE/Jesco von Puttkamer
Subject: <u>Star Trek</u> Convention, Chicago (Trip Report)

Two presentations on "The Future of Manned Space Flight" were given at the <u>Star Trek</u> Convention, 8/22-24, in Chicago. A summary of general personal impressions follows.

The Convention was well organized and smoothly conducted. The exact number of registrants is still being determined at present, but I would estimate it at about 8,000-9,000.* This was an extremely large crowd—even for the giant Conrad Hilton Hotel with its ballrooms and convention halls, all of which appeared filled at all times during the continuous program of activities. My

---

* *The Wall Street Journal* estimated attendance at fifteen thousand.

own presentations (with slides) on 8/22 and 8/23 were attended—on a standing-room-only basis—by about 1,100 people, limited more by size of room than lack of interest. Both presentations were well received and led to long discussions by interested crowds wherever they could manage to corner me . . .

The motivation of the typical *Star Trek* fan seems to go beyond the usual escapism of science fiction fans in general. From the discussions I had, I believe that in many of them the dreams of a *Star Trek* world have heightened the awareness and appreciation of the more immediate future and its positive and negative options for our own world. This having been the first time for me to attend a *Star Trek* convention, what impressed me most is the generally high level of intelligence which I found in many of the people I talked to, their distinctly positivistic and peaceful approach to life, an optimistic outlook on the future, and a general behavior and manner of "gentleness," politeness, and consideration for others . . .

N.A.S.A.'s part in the future was a matter of considerable interest and great enthusiasm. In a formally arranged press conference on 8/21, attended by about 150 press representatives, the only people who drew questions were the *Star Trek* "crew members" and the N.A.S.A. representative. Press coverage was excellent and affirmative in its recognition of the positive values underlying the "movement." Questions in general were intelligent and well-meaning; N.A.S.A.'s interest in getting people's ideas about the future as an "input" in planning was applauded, causing some newsmen later to observe with approval that N.A.S.A. may thus become a "people's agency." The Chicago Tribune of Saturday, 8/23, referred even to "the fabulous N.A.S.A." Jim McDivitt, former astronaut, gave a short presentation on Apollo on 8/23 . . .

I would therefore recommend that we continue to support their efforts as a worthwhile public service and an excellent opportunity to inform this definitely inquisitive sector of the public (which enjoys a good-humored press), availing it with the information and food-for-thought it obviously seeks.

For Manned Space Flight and our own long-range planning efforts, I feel such informal dialogue should be encouraged, and I would be willing to continue supporting it in the future, having also personally enjoyed this experience very much.

      Jesco von Puttkamer
      Advanced Programs, MTE

      5451 Marathon St.
      Hollywood, CA 90038
      Sept. 4, 1975

Dear Mr. von Puttkamer:

Thank you for your letter and most informative copy of your report to N.A.S.A. on the Star Trek convention and phenomenon. It is the best analysis of this subject that I have ever seen.

Appreciate also the attached reports on N.A.S.A. future space-program planning and I will certainly study them carefully. I am a strong advocate of a greatly expanded N.A.S.A. space program and regret that *Star Trek* was not on the air a couple of years earlier, because I believe the phenomenon which developed might have had considerable effect on public attitude toward financing N.A.S.A.'s work. At least, the younger generations of voters who have grown up with *Star Trek* will probably give our space programs strong support when they become the key voting block in our country. We are moving close to that time, since it is noticeable at conventions, as you mentioned, that older fans are now arriving at such gatherings with the "new fan" children.

I hope we can meet, as our mutual friend Fred Durant suggested. We no doubt will have a lot to talk about.

                    Best regards,
                    Gene Roddenberry

Perhaps this is what Anne E. Tetzlaff of Manistee, Michigan, meant when she wrote:

Gene Roddenberry did not just create a show, he created a hope.

One eleven-year-old went so far as to say:

I think Gene Roddenberry is the best producer in the world, and the best creator in the world.

A note written on a tiny slip of paper in a child's handwriting bore this single message:

. . . To boldly go where no man has

gone before. You've done it. You went
up. I really respect your show.

Kris Stack of Binghamton, New York, wrote:

Your dream is coming true! Look at
Apollo-Soyuz!

"Earth is the cradle of the mind," said Tsiolkovsky, "but one cannot live in the cradle forever."

It would seem that Neil Armstrong's "giant leap for mankind" may really be just a toddler's first hesitant steps out of that cradle. Will we stroll among the stars, leaping from quadrant to quadrant of our mysterious galaxy? Gene Roddenberry hopes so. "I think we should be in space," he says. "I think to not go into space would be like Europe sitting over there in the fifteenth century saying 'Why bother with the New World?'" And the STAR TREK fans hope so too. As one fan summarized all our hopes for the future:

Sometimes I feel that I belong with
the Star Trek world, and I wish that I
could live long enough to see those
things happen.

Appendix

Now is the time to get that roll of stamps out and your typewriter and stationery all set. If you are one of the typical fans I mentioned in the Foreword, then this chapter is for you!

The STAR TREK Welcommittee *Fact Sheet* gives the following information, which you may find helpful in answering all your questions about Trekmania:

There is a central information center to answer fans' questions about STAR TREK and to provide new fans with complete information about STAR TREK and STAR TREK fandom. Write to:

> STAR TREK Welcommittee
> Shirley S. Maiewski
> 481 Main Street
> Hatfield, MA 01038

All we ask is a Self-Addressed Stamped Envelope to reply.

STW's monthly report, *A Piece of the Action* (containing current STAR TREK and STAR TREK Fandom news and info, STW business, and occasional feature articles), is available for $5.50 per year from:

> STAR TREK Welcommittee
> P.O. Box 19413
> Denver, CO 80219

STW's 22-page directory, *The Yellow Pages of* STAR TREK (listing clubs, fanzines, books, sale items and conventions), is available for $1.00 from:

> STAR TREK Welcommittee
> Allyson Whitfield
> P.O. Box #206
> New Rochelle, NY 10804

Please always enclose a S.A.S.E. when requesting information.

Teachers wishing further information about STEP (STAR TREK Educational Programs), mentioned in Chapter Six, may write to:

> Mrs. Janice Preston
> In Care of K. J. F.
> 2401 Columbia Pike
> Arlington, VA 22204

Lincoln Enterprises will send you a free catalogue of the STAR TREK merchandise they sell (scripts, film clips, photos, T-shirts, etc.). For the catalogue send a *large* S.A.S.E. to:

> Lincoln Enterprises
> P.O. Box 38429
> Hollywood, CA 90038

An increasing number of schools are now using STAR TREK scripts, writers' guides, and other material in television, cinema, and creative-writing courses. They give a 25 percent discount on all orders of $30 or more received from educational institutions. Orders must meet the following requirements:

1. The order must be received directly from the school on its regular purchase form, or on a letterhead request signed by a member of the teaching or administration staff.
2. Orders from a school should be combined

as much as possible so that Lincoln can make single, rather than multiple, shipments.

3. The orders must specify that you recognize that this is copyrighted material to be used only for nonprofit educational purposes, and that the scripts and other material will not be reproduced or reprinted in any form.

For additional information on *educational discounts*, etc., send a S.A.S.E. to:

> Lincoln Enterprises, Dept. E
> P.O. Box 69470
> Los Angeles, CA 90069

Want to write to your favorite STAR TREK actors? *Don't* write to them at the studio; Publicity takes charge of all fan mail there, and it's likely your letter won't be taken that seriously. *Don't* call us for their home addresses; we won't give these out *under any circumstances* (ditto telephone numbers). The best way to write to the actor/actress is to send the letter in care of his/her official fan club:

> William Shatner Fan Club
> c/o Maxine Lee Broadwater
> 37-51 80th Street
> Jackson Heights, NY 11372

> Leonard Nimoy Assoc. of Fans (LNAF)
> c/o Louise Stange
> 4612 Denver Court
> Englewood, OH 45322

> DeForest Kelley Association of Fans
> c/o Karolyn Popovich
> 1000 South Bryant St.
> Denver, CO 80219

> James Doohan International Fan Club
> c/o Anna Hreha
> 1519 NW 204 St.
> Seattle, WA 98177

George Takei National Fan Club
c/o Mae Sanchez
12028 Millbrook Road
Philadelphia, PA 19154

Walter Koenig Fan Club
c/o Jack Townsend
Rt. #7, Box #295
Lenoir, NC 28645

Nichelle Nichols Fan Club (NNFC)
c/o Virginia Walker
P.O. Drawer #350
Ayer, MA 01432

Majel Barrett Fan Club
c/o Virginia Walker
P.O. Drawer #350
Ayer, MA 01432

Grace Lee Whitney Fan Club
c/o Richard Arnold
P.O. Box 7796
Van Nuys, CA 91409

Mark Lenard * International Fan Club
c/o Sharon Emily
RR #2, Box 100
Washington, IN 47501

---

* He played Sarek, Spock's father.

Acknowledgments

I'd like to thank the people and organizations who helped make this book a reality:

Carole Brownell, Shirley Maiewski, Jeff Maynard, Jon Povill, Majel Roddenberry, Janice Preston, Bjo Trimble, Virginia Walker, Allyson Whitfield, Helen Young, Janet Smith, and Fred Bronson. Also, Lincoln Enterprises, NASA, The STAR TREK Welcommittee, the United States Air Force Academy, and the Washington *Star*.

Special thanks to Cheryl Blythe for helping me through so many crises. Also, my deepest gratitude to Barry McMartin, for suggesting this book.

And my thanks to the hundreds of STAR TREK fans and friends whose letters are used with permission in this book:

Jeannette Abel
Russell Angell
Ernie Ariza
Martin Azarian
Margaret M. Bailey
Sheri Bancroft
Sue Baugh
Joe Bellulovich &
  Valerie Saitas
Dr. Marvin R. Bensman
Sandra J. Berlinski
David C. Berry
Jerry Birdwell
Mari Blakely
Harriet L. Blau
Sheila Dawn Boyer
Dennis R. Brightwell, M.D.
Patricia Brodin
James Brown
Lynn Burgess
Margery Buxbaum
Diane M. Cascello
Ed Chernesky
Kim Chester
Sister Margaret Clarke
John J. Cochran
Daniel Coelho
Mark Cole
Barbara L. Cook, R.N.
Martin Coppola
Donnaray Crouch
David Damico

ACKNOWLEDGMENT

Brian Davis
David Delgado
Brian Deslatte
Kate Devlin
Julie Dickinson & Helen Wood
Joseph DiPirro
F. C. Durant, III
K. A. Ehricke
Richard Elliott
Brent J. Farlie
Amy Foller
Jeffrey Allen Gallus
Robert C. Gartner
George Gerhardt
Robert H. Gibbons
Wanda Gifford
Jason Gold
Margaret Gregory
John R. Guthrie III
Daniel Isaac Guttman
Denny Haberkern
Mrs. D. Haight
Marion Hakes
Wayne Hale
Richard Harman
Bernie Harrison
Stephen M. Herlt
Yoshiko Hirahara
Richard C. Hoagland
Butch Hoover
William Hovespian
David Johnson
Janette Kennedy
Christine V. Kemp
Linky Klapper
Ruth J. Knight
Dean Kolosiek
Danny Lee Kuchynka
Mrs. Charles F. Kull, III
Anthony Kullack
Steve Lacy I
Dr. John Lamb, Jr.

Andrew Langman
Anita Lanzi
John Lazaris
John James Leary
Elise LeBarron
Kip Lee
Rosamond F. Leuty
Sandy Lewis
Thomas Limero
Kevin Lister
Pam Littrell
Jeffrey Alan Lutz
Fern Lynch
Susan MacTavish
Anita Manor
Philip Menza
Beth Miller
Joseph R. Morency
Sandra J. Morse
Barbara Moss
Scott Muench
Sherry Anne Newell
Frank G. Nolte
Robert C. Norris
Chad Oliver
Marilyn Olson
Scott Palmieri
Nancy Paris
Shirley Parker
Diana Pasch
Lisa Patrick
Nathan Payne
April Pentland
Adriana Kfoury Pereira
Juliet Perretti
Greg Pharr
Robert A. Plamondon, Jr.
Bobie Reyes
Ernest Roberts
Edgar M. Rollins
Mary Roswell
W. Edward Roth
Barry Rowell

ACKNOWLEDGMENT 215

Robert Ruiz	Mark Tootle
Diane Sachs	John E. Trybus
Jackie & Joe Seppy	Alex Udell
Stephen Serieka	Allen Van Waggoner
N. Sharpe	Scott Voit
Michael A. Shepherd	Jesco von Puttkamer
Dorrie Silverstone	Brent Wade
David Singer	Glen Walker
George H. Smith	Roy Cameron Walker
John Sole	Virginia Walker
Larry Sommers	Donna Waltz
M. Sperling	Dolores Weinzimmer
Kris Stack	Kenneth R. Westfall
Lee E. Staton	Edward Jay Whetmore
Shelton Stewart	Debbie White
H. C. Sylvester, Jr.	John Wilson
Yoshiko Tamai	The Woodcocks
Tracy Tennant	Brian Yamauchi
Marge Ternus	Atsuko Yokotani
Anne E. Tetzlaff	William J. Zachmeier

and the Great Salt Vampire

ABOUT THE AUTHOR

Susan Sackett was born in New York City and received her master's degree in education at the University of Florida. After moving to California and teaching for a short time, Susan began her career in the media. She spent four years working for NBC, starting as assistant to the National Publicity Manager of "Disney on Parade." It was in this position that she got her start writing. Susan then became Director of Promotions at a small television production company. An auto accident forced her to leave that job, but eight months later—in August 1974—she was hired as Gene Roddenberry's assistant.

Her life has never been the same since!